NAM VET

Making Peace with Your Past

Chuck Dean

NAM VET

Making Peace with Your Past

Chuck Dean

WordSmith Publishing

Published by WordSmith Publishing

Printed in the United States of America.

LCCN #99-62936

Dean, Chuck.

Nam vet: making peace with your / Chuck Dean.

a   cm.

ISBN 0-9679371-0-8

1.Post-traumatic stress disorder-Case studies. 2. Veterans-Mental health-United States-Case studies. 3. Vietnamese Conflict, 1961–1975-Psychological aspects. 4. Vietnamese Conflict, 1961–1975-Personal narratives, American. I. Title. RC552.P67D43 1990 616.85'21-dc20

90-37952

CIP

00 01 02 03 04 05 - 15 14 13 12 11

Contents

CONTENTS

Note: Fictitious names have been used throughout to protect the confidentiality of my brothers-in-arms.

In honor of the 58,178 men and women who gave their lives for their country in S.E. Asia.

*In the service of love . . .
only wounded soldiers can serve.*

They talked softly. They talked of rumors. An observation post by the sea, easy duty, a place to swim and get solid tans and fish for red snapper. Later they talked about going home. It would become a war story. People would laugh and shake their heads, nobody would believe a word. Just one more war story . . .
—Tim O'Brien, *Going After Cacciato*

Everyone Knows a Veteran

They are mail carriers, store clerks, school teachers, attorneys, business owners, airline pilots, your fathers or mothers, husbands or wives. *Nam Vet: Making Peace with Your Past* opens a window to their hidden pain. Its truth will help you be free, because understanding is the first step toward healing.

Here are some readers' comments:

Dear Chuck,

I want to be sure you know what a difference your book has made for the men who come to us for treatment. It must have been both inspiring and healing to write it.

Beverly Donovan, Ph.D.
Veterans Addiction Recovery Center
Veterans Administration
Cleveland, Ohio

ENDORSEMENTS

Chuck,

Can you send me a second copy of *Nam Vet*? My first copy is getting ragged from being passed around so much. All I can tell you is that it has helped me so much to get in touch with my Vietnam experience. The hiding from that time is over for me.

Terry (Nam '66–'67)

Dear Mr. Dean,

I'm a junior in high school and currently doing a term paper on PTSD in Vietnam veterans. I read your book as part of my research and it really struck a chord within me. I never realized what people had to live through, and are still living through now on a daily basis. My father was on an aircraft carrier in Vietnam, and I now understand how it could have affected him badly. Your book helped me to understand many things about what veterans of that war are faced with in their lives today.

A. C.

Chuck,

I just wanted to thank you for taking "point" and writing your book. It's really "our book," ya know? I've looked and listened for so long, knowing that something was wrong inside. I've wasted my life for the last fifteen years, and de-

stroyed a good family life. I've read *Nam Vet* four times now, and nothing has ever helped me face the facts better than it has. It has helped me and my family get back on track . . . there's hope now.

Al (Vietnam '66–'67, SOG)

Nam Vet is an intensely personal book in which Dean bares his life and soul. Because of that, it is one of the more practical, helpful and timely books to hit the shelves in the past few years.

Charles Edgren
El Paso *Herald-Post*

Dear Chuck,

This morning I received a copy (on loan) of your book *Nam Vet* from a mate that served with my unit in Vietnam, who now lives here in West Australia.

After reading only part one of your book I realized that this was the book that I have been looking for. I do voluntary welfare work and since the unveiling of our Vietnam Veterans Memorial in Canberra an increasing number of vets have sought help from us. I don't have all the answers for them, but your book goes all the way in helping them. How can we get more?

Rick Wells
Welfare Officer
Southport Ex-Services Welfare Office
Southport, Australia

Dear Chuck,

A readjustment counselor at the Vets Center gave me your book, *Nam Vet: Making Peace with Your Past.* It is here that I found many expressions similar to my own feelings, including some which I had not heard from other veterans of that war. Your book raises many issues and questions with which I identify. The insightful rationales and suggestions for working through troublesome issues is particularly appreciated. Good luck with your work—it is helping me in my long search for peace of mind.

D. G. (US Special Forces, medic '67–'68)

★ ★ ★ ★ ★

Dear Mr. Dean,

Yesterday I read chapter nine in "Nam Vet." I am keenly, and sometimes painfully, aware that Jesus is preparing me for some rough terrain that lies somewhere not too far ahead of me.

During the ten month delayed entry into the Army, I prayed to God and asked, "Why are You sending me into the Army?" I felt in my spirit that He answered in this way, *Timmy, I've called you to sweat, bleed, and scream with these guys so that on the inside you can share Me with them when the time comes.*

Mr. Dean, God is using the Army to mold and shape me, and He is using your book to prepare my mind, heart and soul for things I may well be exposed to. You probably already know, but God is using you mightily in ministering to my dad's generation as well as to mine.

Sgt. T.N.
U.S. Army Ranger Medic, May, 1999

Foreword

What a wonderful approach. I have read *Nam Vet: Making Peace with Your Past* from cover to cover and appreciate it so much. It led me through many of the thoughts that I have had so very often.

I have left my family four different times to enter combat, each time for more than a year. I was hit by enemy gunfire five times during World War II and often wondered why God was saving me while so many others were being lost. Part of the answer may have been given on my second tour in Vietnam when General Abrams informed me that he was extending my tour a few more months. I did not ask why; I was willing to continue my service without interruption. He then went on to tell me that he had extended me because the figures showed that I was getting the job done. He said every month I stayed in command of my combat unit, he figured about 100 young men lived to go

home who would otherwise have lost their lives. I then
told him that every day I prayed I would do the right thing
by every person who looked for command guidance from
me, and I prayed for my troops.

   Nam Vet is the approach and idea that has been needed
for a long time. I have often said that overcoming psychological problems comes in three stages: (1) convincing the
person that he or she is, in fact, a worthwhile individual;
(2) convincing him that he can do something worthwhile;
(3) sticking with him until he succeeds in accomplishing
something that gives him pride. *Nam Vet* offers all of these,
but most of all, it offers hope for so many who have come
home from Vietnam without it.

ELLIS W. WILLIAMSON
Major General, US Army (Ret)
173d Airborne Brigade Commander Vietnam

CHAPTER 1

"When I Get Home"

★ ★ ★

K IDS BOTHER ME A LOT.
I remember one time when we had just come back from an operation. Things were lax. There was this . . . this kid who came around selling rice wine and sugarcane. He was about twelve or so. I could never tell how old those people were—but he wasn't very old. His bicycle was booby-trapped and suddenly exploded—in our midst. We lost about eight guys there. The worst part of it was that I had to shoot the kid as he was running away—and it was my first kill. If I close my eyes right now I can be there. I didn't want to blow him away. I said, "God, let me hit him where he won't get hurt."

I just wanted to stop him—but what's the use of stopping him? So, for some reason I aimed my rifle at the base of his neck, where I could hit him right in the head. It seems that I held it for hours and hours; it took forever to pull the trigger. But I know it was only a couple of seconds. It all flashed in

front of me in slow motion: the bullet making impact and him
rolling over, becoming a dead heap in the middle of the road.

Now I'll be driving my car, I'll see a little kid, and I imag-
ine . . .

—A combat Marine, in-country 1969

Soon after getting back from Nam, I found myself sleeping
with a K-bar knife under my pillow. I had loaded weapons
around my bedroom and all over the house. I felt it absolutely
necessary. I went through situations where I ended up pulling
these weapons on people because I was startled in the night.

I watch all the time where others are. People scare me be-
cause they don't know that the things they do trip my wire. I'm
afraid I'll react and dust them off without being able to stop
myself. Know what I mean?

Nam is like a cancer—it just keeps eating away at my
insides. I'd like to talk to someone about these things, but I
don't think there's anyone interested in talking about hell. Life
is rose-colored glasses if you've been to Nam. I once tried talk-
ing to a friend about it, but all he gave me was an "under-
standing" smile and a blank look. I'll never do that again be-
cause it made me end up hating him . . . and I've had enough
hate for a lifetime.

—A Vietnam veteran

America's involvement in the war in South Vietnam
ended in 1975. But for thousands of teenagers who did the
fighting, that war lives on as vividly today as it did three
decades ago. While in Nam, the "world" became a revered
and almost mythical place that filled our dreams. We
counted days, hours, minutes, and seconds until we climbed
into our "freedom bird" to return to that world, where all

was safe, all was clean, all was happy. We knew that our war would end as soon as we got back home.

Everyone talked about the world, dreamed about the world, and cried about it. There was nothing more important. The world we sought wasn't some far-off planet—it was our hometowns, our tree-lined streets where we could ride our bikes, our dingy apartments in the ghetto. It was our wives or girlfriends, moms, or any female with round-shaped eyes. The world was where our kid brother lived, and if he ever thought about coming over to this cesspool, we'd personally cut off his trigger finger—for his own good.

The world was refrigerators, toilets that flushed, and swimming holes. It was a magic place that had once existed and would again . . . if only we lived through the next night in Nam. Our only purpose for being there was to make it back to the world, where everything would be sane and normal again.

It didn't happen that way. For most of us, the war never ended. But no one in "the world" can see that but us—and that's the biggest letdown of all. We struggled hard to survive Nam so we could come back into the world we knew and loved. Then, we found out that the world didn't want to hear about Nam or have anything to do with our problems.

Home—the place we thought would be our haven, has become our hell. For more than a quarter of a century, we have suffered as America's "least-favorite minority."

CHAPTER 2

Living for DEROS

★ ★ ★

I F YOU WERE DEMONIC *and powerful enough to want to make someone "crazy" following a war like Vietnam, what would be the worst set of social, economic, political, and psychological conditions you could create for the returnee?*

First, you would send a young man fresh out of high school to an unpopular, controversial guerrilla war far away from home. [You would] expose him to intensely stressful events, some so horrible that it would be impossible to really talk about them later to anyone except fellow "survivors." To ensure maximal stress, you would create a one-year tour of duty during which the combatant flies to and from the war singly, without a cohesive, intact, and emotionally supportive unit with high morale.

You would also create the one-year rotation to instill a "survivor mentality" which would undercut the process of ideological commitment to winning the war and seeing it as a noble cause. Then at DEROS (Date of Expected Return from

Overseas Service), you would rapidly remove the combatant and singly return him to his front porch without an opportunity to sort out the meaning of his experiences with his men in his unit. No homecoming welcome or victory parade.

Since you are demonic enough, you make sure that the veteran is stigmatized and portrayed to the public as a "drug-crazed, psychopathic killer." By virtue of clever selection by the Selective Service System, the veteran would be unable to easily reenter the mainstream of society because he is under-educated and lacks marketable job skills.

. . . Finally, but not least, you would want him to feel isolated, stigmatized, unappreciated, and exploited for volunteering to serve his country.

Tragically, of course, this scenario is not fictitious; it was the homecoming for most Vietnam veterans.

—John F. Wilson in testimony before the US Senate, Committee on Veterans Affairs, 1980

When I was a young paratrooper going through jungle training and various schools to condition my young mind to a war mentality, I dreamed of going to war, winning medals, and protecting our country from evil, invading hordes. Spit-shined jump boots, sparkling brass, and to-the-skin "whitewall" haircuts were the order of the day. I was gung ho, and Vietnam gave me the opportunity to join the ranks of heroes who had gone to war in years past.

I can still remember as a small boy watching with awe the decorated veterans marching in the parades of my small hometown. I wanted so much to be like them, even if it meant losing a leg or an arm. I longed to hear my name—"Dean!"— called off at a morning formation and to be a part of the long, green line. I would be willing, I thought, to suffer through anything. As long as I could be counted in the ranks with the heroes of my country, nothing else mattered.

I was in the advance party of the first US ground troops to launch offensive operations in South Vietnam in 1965. My airborne brigade entered the war with a naivete inspired by John Wayne movies and war stories from Dad or big brother about Korea and the "big one"—World War II. We wanted a piece of that. We wanted to come home in glory, be welcomed into the fold of America's honored warriors.

Like so many other dreams we had, that never happened. The bubble began to burst when we started to get reports that our own people back home didn't want us to fight anymore. Yet we were kept in combat anyway.

In our training on Okinawa, the Philippines, Taiwan, and Irimote, we were "prepared" to kill people who were identified as "the enemy." To accomplish this, the Army employed several psychological tactics. First, they made the enemy less than human to us. "Gooks," "dinks," "zipperheads" were born in our mind and vocabulary. Asians became to us something less than fellow human beings, so we could really "take it to them." We were convinced they were a bunch of soulless heathens—godless creatures who mutilate and destroy and who needed to be dealt with as a menace to the world.

The second step in our preparation to kill other humans involved a motivational tactic—one I personally employed as a drill sergeant when I returned to stateside duty after my tour in Vietnam. We deliberately created rage by instilling the notion that the trainees' wives or girlfriends were out "having a ball" with draft dodgers, hippies, and undesirables, while we soldiers were being isolated in dangerous situations. Recruits were constantly reminded that Jody (a generic term for men who didn't go to war) was sleeping with their women, driving their cars, and even wearing their clothes, while these recruits were away learning to be killers.

With this kind of thought-reform tactic, it's no wonder so many Vietnam veterans are still doubtful and anxious regarding the faithfulness of the women they are married to or are dating. Of course, the fear of losing a wife or girlfriend was not all based in fiction. Many, many soldiers received "Dear John" letters while in-country, and 38 percent of soldiers who were married prior to leaving for Vietnam, were divorced within six months after returning home. I'm not proud of the fact that I've been divorced twice, and it's only by the grace of God that my third marriage is a happy and surviving relationship.

The Never-Ending War

Concerned relatives and friends of Nam vets find it difficult to understand why the war seems so unending for "Johnny," who was a nice kid back when. One of the most common questions these people ask is, "Why was Vietnam so different from Korea or World War II?"

Many nonveterans list glib reasons to explain why we veterans are so screwed up. Most boil down to a familiar jingle: "The poor Vietnam vet never got a parade or welcome home after the war. All of the war protests were really cruel. That's why these guys are so warped." While the first two statements are true, to believe this is the root of the problem is foolish.

I believe there are at least six major reasons the Vietnam War was psychologically damaging to many of our soldiers and support personnel. The first is that we were trained to dehumanize, hate, and kill with no debriefing before returning home. We've already looked at this briefly. The other five reasons for our postwar maladjustment are described in the balance of this chapter and the one that follows.

DEROS: It Seemed Like a Great Idea

Every man and woman who went to Vietnam knew when he or she would be coming home. For almost everyone, it was twelve months after arriving (the Marines were on thirteen-month tours). This rotation system was called DEROS (date of expected return from overseas).

DEROS promised us a way out of the war, without becoming a physical or psychological casualty. As our DEROS approached, we became short-timers, holding ourselves together for a few more months so we could get back to the world and leave the war far behind. It appeared to be a great plan, but it failed utterly, creating a root to the readjustment problems that have grown worse over the years.

DEROS was a very personal thing. It created an individualistic attitude in us. Each person's war began when he arrived in-country. It ended on his DEROS. For every Vietnam veteran, DEROS was the fantasy that on one predetermined day—in that golden moment when he boarded an airliner back to the States—all of his problems would end. Each American knew that when he got home, everything would become normal again, that he would be respected and acknowledged for services he had rendered.

When a young "troop" arrived in-country, he wasn't briefed on any of the war strategies or even about where he'd be living for the next year. Instead, he was usually told he was assigned to such-and-such a unit, up at some gobbledygook place. "So get on the chopper, Cherry, and make it snappy!"

He immediately began to seek out a purpose, a stable point in the midst of all the terror and confusion. Most found only one: to stay alive for 365 days. He wasn't there to beat the Commies or even to win a war. He wanted only to get to his DEROS in one piece. This rotation system caused any ideology that Vietnam was a "good fight" to quickly desist among the troops. The war effort and reasons for the war could go to hell as far as we were concerned.

I was luckier than the guys who came later. I didn't have to be a new guy. Since we were the first troops in Vietnam, we were all "greenies" or "cherries." Paratroopers are known for a strong esprit de corps, and we had a lot of pride in our unit. The DEROS system quickly undermined our pride and slashed our esprit considerably, after only a few months in-country. It continued to demoralize the entire military structure for the duration of the war.

Instead of building strength through common team objectives, each unit became a revolving door of personnel coming and going. The most important maneuver of the war was to get home and become normal again. Our heroes weren't the guys winning medals or the ones out humping the bush; they were the ones with the shortest time left to serve in the war. We praised them, and short-timers overtly mocked us with how wonderful and carefree life would be as soon as they returned home.

By the end of a tour, most everyone couldn't care less about what unit he had been with for the past year. His closest friends were usually only a handful of buddies in a squad or platoon, and unit history and tradition were something that only "lifers" (career soldiers) could get into. Years later, in their search for answers to their problems, a lot of vets have had to dig around in libraries to find any background data on the unit with which they had served.

I was recently at a memorial with about sixty-five hundred other Vietnam veterans. During the day's events, two hundred or so bikers in leathers, colors, tattoos, Harleys, and all, paraded their bikes into our midst. Although they looked almost exactly like Hell's Angels, they were not. The back of their denim and leather jackets read "Vietnam Veterans." We greeted each other with hugs and tears, becoming one once again. These men had been riding together for many years and had finally found some unit pride.

A pastor from a local church who was there to help with any spiritual needs, asked me why so many Nam vets went into motorcycle gangs when they came home. I was disturbed because I couldn't answer his question. So I talked with many veterans who either had ridden with a motorcycle club or been affiliated with one since they'd returned from Nam. It wasn't long before I detected a loyalty and pride that seemed very similar to what I'd seen as a prewar paratrooper.

What unit esprit and pride these guys had missed in Vietnam, they instantly obtained in their membership in these hard-riding clubs. The lack of any group dynamic during the war was quickly satisfied by the strong bonds of brotherhood they found in a group they could identify with, a group that readily accepted them. Our country, in general, didn't accept them or acknowledge their hard-earned abilities to kill and to survive. But bikers did. This unqualified acceptance was an easy way to come home.

During the war, many vets became so accustomed to carrying weapons that it was difficult to be away from them when they returned to the States. For many years I wouldn't go anywhere without my pistol, either tucked in the back of my pants or under the driver's seat in my car. Since motorcycle clubs, such as the Hell's Angels, tend to live a hardcore life, weapons are commonplace. Here again, this was an easy transition for the Nam vet to make.

Short-Timer's Syndrome

When a seasoned "troop" got down to his last couple of months in Vietnam, he became overpowered by the strange fantasy of being a short-timer. What developed was short-timer's syndrome. This soldier was typically withdrawn from all field duty and taken to a relatively safe base camp for the rest of his tour. He left his unit with ambivalent emotions of joy and guilt, because he knew that his companions, whom he was leaving behind, relied on his skills to survive. He was replaced by a new guy who was unskilled, often literally thrown from a chopper into the unit of seasoned "troops."

DEROS always kept one "troop" coming and one going. The one coming began marking days until it was over. The one leaving had a gnawing feeling that he had unfinished business and had completed a purposeless year of his young life, playing with automatic weapons, hand grenades, and claymore mines.

One teenage soldier stated it this way:

> The year others knew as youth, I spent learning the meaning of death. The times others spent learning to love, I passed hoping to live through endless nights. The moments others remember as laughs in classrooms, I remember as terror in the jungle. The instants of pleasure taken for granted by others, I remember as forgotten hopes . . . long ago crushed by the reality of war. The unfulfilled dreams of others are yet to be thought by me since I am in search of my elusive youth, looking for years lost in combat, which are no more . . . and will never be.

We also looked at DEROS as our deliver-us-from-evil system. We thought our departure date would spring us from the morass, from the evil moral jungle of Vietnam.

We knew that as soon as we got home, our parents would be proud of us, our friends would be happy, and everything would be marvelous.

For many of us, the idea that we had come home without any major wounds was one of the greatest deceptions of the war. Our wounds were invisible, at first. We held our spiritual darkness and psychological confusion inside, and nobody but us veterans knew it was there. It seems that vets who received serious physical wounds—especially amputees—made the transition back better than those of us with no apparent wounds. One reason for this is that medical personnel generally recognized that physical wounds would cause readjustment problems. Disabled veterans were given extensive psychological assistance to prepare them for the new life they faced back home.

On the other hand, those of us who had no apparent wounds were loaded on a jet (many times right out of a firefight or mortar attack) and thirty hours later found ourselves walking around a busy American airport. We had no debriefing. We were all alone, trying to cope with normal American life again. That set us up to perpetuate the isolationism, which we thought we had just escaped.

The Way It Happened to Me

My DEROS was pretty typical. I turned in my weapons and gear at Bien Hoa, was trucked to Saigon's Tan Son Nhut Airport, and proceeded to get drunk in a small barbed-wire compound that was set up for us. My war was over, and I began to let loose of all the stress I'd stuffed away over the past two years. (I'd spent a year on Okinawa before Vietnam.)

We were to leave at 0600 the next morning, and we drank beer until about 0300 hours. I had just flopped on a cot inside a small shack, when the VC began to mortar the helicopters on a pad next to our tiny compound. They missed the choppers and hit us instead. Seven guys died just three hours before boarding their "freedom bird."

I battle-dressed shrapnel wounds on my arm and rolled my sleeves down so no one would see that I had been hit. There was no way I was going to take a chance of being medically detained from leaving at 0600. As far as I was concerned, they could give my Purple Heart to one of the dead guys' parents; I wasn't missing my flight.

I'll never forget landing at Travis Air Force Base in California. My mouth must have gaped wide when I saw the manicured lawns, clean streets, and women who were as tall as I. The airport at San Francisco was equally awesome and mysterious. A young couple passed by me, talking about buying a new refrigerator. Someone else was talking about driving up through the Redwoods, and a student with long hair was packing his skis. Not one person I saw was on the alert for danger, and no one seemed to know or care that my friends were humping the bush and dying in rice paddies and jungles that very night.

My plane touched down at the Seattle-Tacoma Airport. I disembarked and went inside. My mother walked right past me in the terminal. She didn't even recognize me. I stood and watched her without saying a word. At that moment, I knew life was not going to be the way I'd dreamt about it as a short-timer in the Iron Triangle.

CHAPTER 3

A Different Kind of War

★ ★ ★

I GOT SENT TO SAIGON *to pull guard duty on a supply convoy. In front of the capitol building, its half-inch-thick gold plating shining brightly in the morning sun, a dirty, ragged horde of kids swarmed around our trucks. They screamed for us to throw C-rations to them. The contrast between the building's untold wealth and these kids' unspeakable poverty ripped at my heart.*

"—— you, GI." "Go home, GI." "Tonight you die, GI." "VC kill you, GI." These were about all the English words the kids knew how to say, never comprehending their meaning. The Communist cadre was teaching kids that these were the words to use to get food from us. It was part of the war against us, totally unreal. As they reached out and tugged at our pants, their grins proclaimed a message different from the words they mouthed. Their eyes begged, "Help me, GI."

—A Vietnam veteran

Vietnam was a different kind of war. At the time, we didn't know it. We thought every war was supposed to be like Nam. I remember one day when a four year old wandered into a crowd of soldiers to beg for food. His eyes sparkled when we gave him something to eat. Then he exploded into pieces from the satchel charge he never knew was on his back. Booby-trapping innocent children didn't seem like the way war was supposed to be fought.

Every Vietnam veteran probably has at least one of these gut-wrenching, eyewitness accounts lodged in his or her memory. And most nonveterans have heard some bizarre stories about the tactics used on innocents over there. But in my view, it was primarily the subtle hypocrisies of the military management that made Vietnam a different kind of war.

CHAIRBORNE COMMANDOS

Throughout our prewar training, we were drilled on the effectiveness of counterguerrilla warfare and why it was very important to move about with the guerrilla, instead of digging into a stationary position. We learned that the guerrilla is a free spirit who moves about at will. If you don't move with him, you then become his target—and he'll pick the time and place to clobber you.

The French lost to the Viet Minh (forerunners to the Viet Cong) because they fought a fixed war. They built brick fortresses, strung barbed wire around them, and fought the war from these strongholds. The guerrillas had complete access to the food supplies of the countryside, to the people, and to virtually the entire nation at night. The French fought during the daylight hours and retreated to their fortresses at night. The Viet Minh were always in control because they melted into the population during the day and ran unchecked at night.

During our long months preparing for Vietnam, the French mistakes were used as classic examples of how not to fight a guerrilla war. We were to get out there in the bush and stay there—day and night. Our objective was to take the night away from the enemy.

My unit, the 173d Airborne Brigade, was one-of-a-kind in the military history of this country. It was the only military unit that never set foot on American soil during its entire life. The brigade was formed on Okinawa and retired in Vietnam at the end of the war. Since we were the reactionary force for Asia, we were the first to go to Vietnam in 1965.

The 173d was designed to be very mobile. Therefore, every trooper was a combatant, regardless of whether he was a typist, mechanic, or cook. When the unit went into action, everybody was on the line. There was no carpet that you could crawl under, no safe, air-conditioned rear area.

For the first few months, the 173d ran "Charlie" (the enemy) ragged. We were out there doing what we were supposed to do to fight a guerrilla war. But things began to change as more American units steadily arrived in-country. The top brass in Saigon built big bases, and the "security blanket" syndrome set in. The Viet Cong and North Vietnamese Army began to control the night. The 173d became less and less effective as a STRAC unit; we were swallowed up in "chairborne commando" strategies.

The very thing America vowed not to do—build big bases and defend them—became the order of the day. Cam Ranh Bay, Bien Hoa, An Khe, DaNang (the list goes on) were all superwar cities that America created, cities from which to fight the Communists. They were also dens of sin. Drugs, prostitution, black marketeering, and gambling were only a few of the open vices that ran rampant in these big camps. These fleshpots were not only nests of corruption, but they also provided a sanctuary for the soldier who did not want to expose himself to the dangers and hardships of combat.

At the peak of America's involvement, the total number of troops committed to Vietnam was 500,000. Fewer than 50,000 were engaged in fighting in the field; 450,000 men and women were in the security defense of these big bases. We didn't lose the war because we were poor soldiers in the field; we were good. We couldn't win because so few of us actually got out there to do what we were trained to do.

The whole "American Vietnam" became a scenario of a few men fighting and the majority looking for a way to get stoned, laid, on R-&-R or to make quick money. The guys in the field carried the war load, but they dreamed of getting back to a "rear area."

Career soldiers who had spent most of their time at the Pentagon would sign up for a tour in Vietnam so they could win some decorations. Some would wheedle a deal to get stationed at these big, secure bases; stay for six months; and come home with Bronze Stars, Silver Stars, or whatever. Few of them ever spent a wet night in the bush looking for the enemy. With their medals on the records, they could receive future promotions. "American Vietnam" became their safe, easy way to get them.

The hard-won medals of those few guys out in the field, engaging "Charlie," became an insignificant joke. To be honored for heroism was nearly a humbug.

Defense is only a temporary tactic at best, especially in a guerrilla war. It should be a posture that a combat unit takes to regroup, attend the wounded, and plan the next attack. In Vietnam, defense was the way things were, and the communists continued to chew into our defense at will. No war in history was ever won from within four walls.

Real-Estate Agents vs. Conquest

In one way, Vietnam was much like all other wars the United States has ever fought. It was a war of sending troops into an area for the purpose of gaining ground. The only problem with this strategy was that it was absolutely the wrong way to fight that war.

In World War II, Hitler and the Allies were fighting to control the same objective: territory. Vietnam was something like a contest between a baseball team and a football team. The Communists were trained to fight for an idea; we were trained to fight for territory or physical objectives. The Viet Cong couldn't have cared less about occupying a certain location. They were fighting for the liberation of their brothers from capitalist domination. We were fighting to occupy a certain hill or rice paddy. They were fighting for minds, we for ground. We repeatedly secured the same terrain objectives at a great expense of lives. The enemy would get us to concentrate on winning a hill or area, then disappear when they felt like it. They sucked us into the game of wasting time, lives, and taxpayers' money by showing themselves as an occupying force on a certain geographical location. We would accept the challenge and play king of the mountain while they laughed and sent a few more tons of ammunition down the Ho Chi Minh Trail, uncontested.

When we eventually became apathetic about winning a "ground" war, the only measure that we had left to indicate progress was the "body count" of reported enemy dead. If a patrol killed two enemy troops in an ambush, it was believed that approximately twenty more were actually killed, because the North Vietnamese army was notorious for carrying off their dead. Body count became the biggest farce in Vietnam. It was a way to keep score and to tally up medals that the brass put themselves in line to receive.

We were in Vietnam to help the South Vietnamese win a war against Communism. That's what we were told. But it was strange to be fighting for a country of people who didn't like us. At any given time, I could go out into a rice paddy and ask *Papasan* who he wanted to win the war. He would have answered, "I don't care. All I want is to grow my rice and be left alone." I knew something was wrong when we threw C-rations over the sides of the trucks to the people, and they threw them back at us with the intention of doing harm. The two realities—fighting for the freedom of a hostile people—didn't mesh.

It became clear to us (while still in combat or upon arriving home) that our country and commanders had betrayed us. We felt lied to about the purpose of most of the things we were ordered to do. We felt lied to about the promised glory and veteran benefits after returning home. Our cynicism toward the government, God, nonveterans, and the American way of life usually began when, as young vets, we stepped off the plane. We knew things weren't going to be the same as when we left.

Probably the single most devastating thing for us was the "scapegoating" this country generally heaped on the Vietnam returnee. Not only did we come home with a good case of survivor's guilt (feelings of guilt because we survived combat, while close friends did not), but also student activists, the press, and a lot of churches generated a moral guilt, which made us acutely aware that our personal actions in the war were wrong. We were made to believe that the war was evil and we should not have participated in it. We got this message from the very same people who had sent us to do for our country what they themselves weren't willing to do.

WHY IT WASN'T LIKE EUROPE OR JAPAN

Perhaps the best way to illustrate the difference between the Vietnam War and previous wars is to compare the lives of soldiers in both. This will move us from generalities to specifics.

Consider an eighteen-year-old boy in 1942. He went off to war in Europe, sticking with his unit for an extended time and making many friends. Together, they ended up in France. The unit fought the war on the battlefront, and our young soldier always knew that the enemy was in front of him. He also knew that the French people were behind him. They loved him and considered him a liberator. His unit fought until it was replaced by another unit. Then he and his surviving companions were moved to the rear (usually Paris) for rest. After the war, he and thousands of other soldiers loaded onto troop ships and spent a couple of weeks floating back across the Atlantic. During this time, they debriefed each other about their wartime experiences. It was their decompression chamber from the war, giving them time to wind down and get their thinking straight. They arrived home, all disembarking at one location. They marched off the troop ships into a New York City ticker-tape parade and were welcomed back once and for all.

Now let's look at another eighteen-year-old, this one drafted in 1967 and sent off to Vietnam. After sixteen weeks of training, he was sent home on a leave before going overseas. Then he reported in, alone, to a marshaling point on the West Coast. There, he was loaded into a commercial jetliner and swooped across the Pacific in less than thirty hours. Arriving in Saigon, he got jostled along to pick up jungle gear, loaded onto a helicopter, and airlifted out to a jungle base-camp where he was dumped off. There, he became a "new guy." None of the seasoned "troops" even wanted to know his name, other than "new guy" or "cherry." New guys had a bad habit of stepping on mines and booby traps and getting maimed or killed—along with everyone around them. Keeping a good distance from a "cherry" was accepted policy.

This teenage soldier was never sure of anything he was doing. He wasn't briefed on war strategies or instructed on exactly who were the enemy. He found that the South Vietnamese people (whom he was sent to help) disliked and ridiculed him, even while they expected him to fight the war for them as they played games on the black market. His prime purpose for being in Vietnam changed from that of winning the war, to that of surviving 365 days so he could go home and forget this nightmare.

Somewhere along the line, he became a seasoned "troop" himself, only because he lived long enough to be called that by others. His one year in-country finally came to an end. He was extracted from the bush by helicopter and then jetted out of Vietnam. He arrived back in the States in less than thirty hours. There, he received no debriefing, no decompression time, no parades, and he encountered no friends who understood the experience he'd gone through for the last twelve months. He found himself alone in a country that couldn't care less that he'd spent his eighteenth birthday in a leech-infested rice paddy, scared half to death that he was about to die.

COMPARISON OF VIETNAM WAR STRESSES WITH OTHER WARS

Following is a list of stresses typical for all wars:

1. Miserable living conditions
2. Fatigue

3. Sensory assault
4. The fighting itself
5. Wounds
6. Special stresses of the combat situation
7. Capture and torture
8. Isolation
9. Acute survivorship (surviving when all others are killed)
10. Authoritarian organization
11. Command incompetence
12. The observers (fighting while others merely watched)

The next list includes unusual stresses peculiar to the Vietnam War:

1. Guerrilla warfare
2. Lack of clear objectives
3. Limitations in offensive actions
4. Terrorism (all of Vietnam was a combat zone, no rear area)
5. Climate and typography
6. Miscellaneous, bizarre physical dangers
7. Tropical diseases
8. Immersion in an extraordinarily poor third-world society
9. Chaos and confusion
10. Psychological/political stresses
11. Experience of absurd waste
12. Government deceit and misjudgment
13. Massive national conflict (undeclared war, etc.)
14. Defeat

HIGH-TECH KIDS AND TOYS

The average age of the World War II soldier was twenty-four. For Americans in Vietnam, it was eighteen. It was the first teenage war the United States ever fought. When most kids that age should have been souping up their cars or going to Saturday-night dances, these kids were playing with M-16 fully automatic rifles, fragmentation grenades, and plastic explosives.

We were the offspring of the soldiers who fought in World War II and Korea. We were a generation of warrior's kids and were expected to make a war out of Vietnam the way all other American wars had been fought. But this was a high-tech war, a testing ground for new war ideas, and we were high-tech kids in a state of confusion.

I look at my sons and try to imagine them operating an M-16 rifle. They are the same age as most of the guys who fought in Vietnam. Although I now have one son who is a paratrooper with the 82nd Airborne Division, it is tough to imagine him using such a weapon to kill people.

The technology put into the M-16 was something else. The 5.56-millimeter round it fired was no ordinary bullet. It was extremely small compared to the old M-1 or M-14 round, and it had an interesting characteristic. Instead of simply making a hole in something (or someone) and exiting out the back, it would enter the target and explode. On impact, the bullet would tumble, shattering and tearing anything it contacted. If it hit you in the leg, it might exit out your neck area, pulling your intestines out with it. That was a teenage toy.

THE WAR THAT DIDN'T END

The statistics on the war's after effects on Vietnam veterans seem to change every time I turn around. I've gathered the following from the Veterans Administration, the Disabled American Veterans, and Trauma Recovery, Inc. These alone give evidence that Vietnam was a different kind of war.

1. Of those veterans who were married before going to Vietnam, 38 percent were divorced within six months after returning from Southeast Asia.
2. The divorce rate for all Vietnam veterans is in the ninetieth percentile.
3. Between 40 and 60 percent of all Vietnam veterans have persistent problems with emotional adjustment.
4. The suicide rate among veterans who have completed the local VA program is estimated at 2.5 per hundred. The national accidental death and suicide rate is fourteen thousand men per year—33 percent above the national average.
5. Fifty-eight-thousand-plus Americans died in the Vietnam War. Over 150,000 have committed suicide since the war ended.
6. Five hundred thousand Vietnam veterans have been arrested or incarcerated by the law. It is estimated that there are 100,000 Vietnam vets in prison today and 200,000 on parole.
7. Drug- and alcohol-abuse problems range between 50 percent and 75 percent.
8. Forty percent of Vietnam veterans are unemployed and 25 percent earn less than seven thousand dollars per year.

These statistics point to a major problem—a problem the people of America cannot afford to ignore too much longer. While they may not want to listen to us, our statistics will be heard. But it doesn't have to be that way. Let's shift our focus from what went wrong thirty years ago, to where we're at today. I believe there is real help available, though it may not come from the quarter you expect.

CHAPTER 4

The Price Still Being Paid

★ ★ ★

IHAD STUFFED THAT MEMORY *somewhere beyond availability.* ● ● ● *I carried that night around within me for over a decade. Never consciously remembering it . . . yet I had never really let go of it. I was bound by it . . . like living on the edge of a nightmare, I was afraid to let myself feel or experience. I couldn't tell anyone this. No one would ever understand, so who would believe me? You know, you don't really live while something like that sits inside you.*

—A Vietnam veteran of 1967–1968

When healing is denied the body or mind of a human being, wounds remain exposed, open, and raw. Without the natural process of change and adaptation, these wounds fester. We Vietnam veterans have watched our physical wounds heal. The scars left on our flesh remind us of our former pain and suffering. But the wounds in our minds have become wounds in our spirits as well. To simply say, "What happened in Vietnam, happened. End of story," is a gross denial of our deep, inner craving for authentic spiritual truth and psychological healing.

Many of us suffer from the aftereffects of having been in heavy combat and under direct fire. (I personally believe considerable healing occurs when a sufferer truly finds a worthwhile reason or purpose for his suffering and pain.) A lot of vets have serious identity problems and a sense of spiritual alienation that leads us into repeated destructive and self-destructive symptoms and behaviors. We are particularly vulnerable to exhibiting severe symptoms of what is known as post-traumatic stress disorder, commonly called PTSD.

Psychologists have surmised that the stress manifestations of the Vietnam War are the same as those found in POWs of the Korean War and in atomic-blast survivors of Hiroshima. Listen to this testimony from Dr. John P. Wilson of Cleveland State University's department of psychology, given before a US Senate Subcommittee on Veteran Affairs, May 21, 1980:

> We know now that PTSD is a dynamic survivor response to the catastrophic stressors experienced in the war and to the intense social stressors after it. The symptoms which define the PTSD syndrome among Vietnam veterans are virtually identical to those observed among the survivors of the atomic bomb at Hiroshima, Korean POW camps, the Nazi holocaust, and the Buffalo Creek Dam disaster.

Our all-pervasive emotional and spiritual problems are related to PTSD, and they interfere with our ability to lead meaningful and productive lives.

Unlike the shell-shock problem of veterans from other wars, PTSD is found both in combat veterans and in many rear-echelon, support-type troops. It has been diagnosed in sailors who spent their entire tours off the coast on ships. It has been found in troops who were in Thailand supporting the war from that country. Post-traumatic stress disorder is a widespread burden, packed around inside the minds and hearts of the majority of Vietnam veterans, regardless of our job or proximity to danger.

To recognize PTSD as a real, unimagined part of the war's aftereffects is vital, not only for us veterans, but also for all of our "significant others" (family members, close friends, employers, etc.). In order to find healing, we and the people closest to us need to understand and accept that this condition is genuine. PTSD is not a mental illness. It is a reaction to the extreme stress we encountered during the war and upon returning home. And we need to find a worthwhile purpose for all of our years of pain and suffering.

A Diagnosis Long in Coming

At first, there seemed to be no explanation for Vietnam veterans having the multitude of problems we have. Our suicide rate jumped to 33 percent above the national average. Criminal convictions and alcohol and substance abuse were way out of proportion with any other group in America. People protesting the war used statistics about these symptoms to verify their soapbox belief that the war was disgusting and America shouldn't be involved in it. Others who supported the war used veterans' problems as evidence of the brutal, dirty tactics of the Communists, finding more justification for the morality of their prowar position. In the meantime, ailing veterans—unattended—took the brunt of another political mixed bag.

It was not until the early 1980s that scientific studies began to reveal the true nature of PTSD. Only then was it even given a proper name among the scientific and governmental communities, which had to confront the complaints about the severity of the illness. (They couldn't deny the problem anymore in light of the fact that 72 percent more soldiers killed themselves after returning home from Vietnam than died in hostile fire during the war.)

Our psychological, physical, and spiritual problems were generally misunderstood by doctors and clergy in this country. These professionals often showed a lax attitude about the severity of our symptoms. Obviously, as people trained and conditioned to survive constant life-threatening experiences, our adjustment to normal social life was difficult, nearly impossible. We had done and seen things that made coming back to "business as usual" practically unobtainable. Our country, however, did not see it that way.

Recently, a friend told me about his return from Vietnam. He had survived the most brutal battle of the entire war, slugging out his very soul in combat, and had been spat upon when he arrived at the San Francisco Airport. After two days, his father threatened to kick him out because he didn't have a job yet. "Business as usual" to dad was working eight hours a day and getting paid for it. For the son, it was a helicopter ride into the bush, sleepless nights of watching for an elusive enemy coming through the barbed wire, and trying not to be killed.

MAJOR SYMPTOMS OF PTSD

There are a number of primary PTSD responses we exhibit as a result of our experiences in Southeast Asia and back in the United States (or Canada). Psychologists and psychiatrists working with the Disabled American Veterans Outreach Program compiled the list that follows. Most Vietnam veterans show only a few of these responses. The major PTSD responses are

1   Depression
2   Cynicism and distrust of government and authority
3   Anger
4   Alienation
5   Sleep disturbances
6   Concern with humanistic values overlaid by hedonism
7   Tendency to react under stress with survival tactics
8   Psychic or emotional numbing
9   Negative self-image
10 Memory impairment
11 Emotional constriction
12 Hypersensitivity to justice
13 Loss of interest in work and activities
14 Problems with intimate relationships
15 "Survivor guilt"
16 Difficulty with authority figures
17 Hyperalertness
18 Avoidance of activities that arouse memories of traumas in war zone
19 Emotional distance from children, wife, and others
20 Self-deceiving and self-punishing patterns of behavior, such as an inability to talk about war experiences, fear of losing others, and a tendency to fits of rage
21 Suicidal feelings and thoughts
22 Flashbacks to Vietnam
23 Fantasies of retaliation and destruction

A few of these delayed stress responses may sound familiar to you and the people closest to you. But you and they may even deny these reactions when they appear. There are other telling clues that you may be suffering from PTSD. Let's rerun through a number of the reactions, looking at a few specific ways they might be expressed in your daily life.

Intrusive thoughts and flashbacks. Do you replay combat experiences in your mind, searching for alternate outcomes? Do everyday experiences trigger flashbacks—things such as, the sound of helicopters; the smell of urine or diesel fuel; the odor of mold or smell of Asian foods being cooked; green tree lines; popcorn popping or a car backfiring; rainy days; seeing refugees?

Isolation. Do you have very few friends? Do you attempt to isolate yourself from family members either emotionally or geographically? Do you have a leave-me-alone attitude toward your loved ones or feel that you need no one? Do you sometimes fantasize about becoming a hermit, moving away from your problems? Do you believe no one can understand you or would listen if you tried to talk about your experiences?

Emotional numbing. Do you see youself as cold, aloof, uncaring, and detached? Do you often fear losing control, or that if you began to release your pain, you might never stop crying? Are you concerned about your emotional distance from your children or about how strongly you show your anger toward them?

Depression. Do you often feel helpless, worthless, and dejected? Are you usually feeling insecure? Do your good feelings seem undeserved? Are you sometimes unable to handle it when things are going well, and do you try to sabotage your success or well being?

Anger. Do you take out your anger upon inanimate objects? Upon loved ones? Are you subject to a quiet, masked rage, which frightens you and those around you? Are you unable to identify or handle things that frustrate you? Is your anger unexplainable or inappropriate—excessive to the situation? Do you believe God abandoned you in Vietnam?

Substance abuse. Do you use alcohol or drugs regularly? Do they numb your pain and memories or relieve your guilt? Do others think you rely upon liquor or drugs too much?

Guilt, suicidal feelings and thoughts. Do you regularly wonder why you survived when others more worthy than you died? Do you get into hopeless fights or give blood excessively? Have you had a lot of "accidents" with power tools? As soon as things are going well financially, do you do something to lose it all—or walk away from it?

Anxiety and nervousness. Are you startled by cans popping, fireworks, and other loud noises? Do these sounds jettison you into a state of combat readiness? Are you uncomfortable when people walk closely behind you or sit behind you? Are you generally suspicious of others? Do you feel you can trust no one?

Emotional constriction. Are you unable to talk about personal emotions? Do you find it impossible to achieve intimacy with your family, partner, or friends? Do you repress feelings?

Some of these symptoms of PTSD may hit pretty close to home. In fact, I may have just tripped your wire. If so, put the book down and come back to it when you're ready to continue. You may feel pressured or that your feelings are writhing inside of you. Stay with me. There is a way out.

FAILURE OF THE VA PROGRAMS

One part of the traditional treatment for Vietnam veterans is in a sad situation. Secular counseling has pronounced PTSD as an incurable commodity we've earned for serving our country as we did. In fact, some PTSD problems are considered untreatable in many of us.

I once heard a fellow vet describe the Veterans Administration solutions to his problem. He said it was "like putting a Band-Aid over a bullet hole." They could cover it up, but they couldn't stop the bleeding.

VA counseling and rap (discussion) groups have allowed many of us to open up some deeply rooted emotional scars. To a degree, it has been good to get some of these untold horrors and nightmares off our chests by telling them to a group of peers. The problem is that we soon become a sort of nut in the rap-group squirrel cage. There seems to be no rhyme or reason for continuously probing these long-buried wounds. The psychiatric world has no solid answers for curing PTSD. There are no tenable solutions coming from the secular community.

Lack of family and community support, inadequate aftercare, unclear treatment goals, and adversarial relationships between veterans and health-care providers seem to be the major causes for the break down of government programs. For us, our bleeding beneath the proverbial Band-Aid has developed into a bitterness that seems to seethe just below the boiling point, a bitterness directed toward the VA and all government authority. We carry a widespread mistrust and sense alienation, and many suffering vets have walked away from secular programs, believing that "I'm just screwed up, and that's the way it will be the rest of my life."

The Vietnam War was the longest war in our country's history. With abundant high-tech medical attention rapidly deployed in the field by helicopters, we had more war survivors than America experienced in any other war. There were over eight million people in the armed forces during the Vietnam War; 2.8 million were combatants. Only 58,178 died, and 2,413 are still missing (as compared with around 290,000 killed in World War II, with over 12,000 listed as missing in action). That leaves us with millions of survivors in dire need of psychological and spiritual help.

I know that PTSD can be licked. My trauma was brought into "remission" over a decade ago. Now I'm giving my time, strength, and resources to help brothers, such as you, find release and final healing for this inner sickness.

In the following pages, we'll walk through ways to handle the seven most prevalent responses to PTSD.

CHAPTER 5

"It Don't Mean Nothin'"

★ ★ ★

JOHN SAT DOWN IN an exhausted heap. The red dust puffed up as he leaned back on his heavy rucksack and pulled a cigarette from a small plastic container he kept stuck it the camouflage band around his helmet.

The long hours of the battle for Hue City had lulled into a sudden stillness, leaving the soldiers of the 101st Airborne wondering if the 1968 Tet Offensive was over. They hoped it was, because the low cloud-cover had prevented them any access to air support from navy jets. And "Charlie" had been pounding them unmercifully with everything he had.

Looking around through tired, eighteen-year-old eyes, John witnessed the carnage of a once-beautiful Asian city. Not one building had escaped being riddled with millions of pockmarks from bullets and shrapnel. The city was a complete shambles. Across the open square in front of him lay *dead, mangled people and cattle. Cries of pain and wails of grief came from every direction.*

The 120-degree sun already was boiling the putrid odors of decaying flesh and excrement into his nostrils, and he felt a helplessness engulf him. It was as if he had fallen into a dream, with no control to stop it. There was nothing he could do about where he was or what was going on around him. He must have already died and gone to hell, he reasoned, and this was what it was like there. It was the only logical answer for what he was experiencing, but what had he done to deserve being there? All seemed lost in that moment. His life could never be the same.

That was one young trooper's experience after a hard-fought battle in Vietnam. It is also a classic example of how many veterans were inflicted with the post-traumatic stress symptom of depression. Depression is accompanied by a crippling sense of helplessness. It's tough for a veteran to climb out of that hole, especially when he feels no one would ever understand the sorrow, guilt, anger, and pain he has witnessed or is currently feeling.

In the case of John, the ravages of the battle in Hue City brought on his depressed state. He is still haunted by the effects of those terrible hours in 1968. A few years ago, he was working as a welder at a Seattle shipyard and happened to be in conversation with a couple of younger men who had not been in Nam. He was telling them about the cloud-cover over Hue, which had kept air support from taking part in the battle. It was a cloudy day in Seattle, which is not unusual, and while relating the story to his friends, John felt a sudden rush of panic. He fell immobilized on the deck of the ship on which they were working and had to leave work to recuperate from the shock of his "flashback."

What Is Depression?

Depression is a difficult to define, even more difficult to treat, yet one of the most common afflictions known to humans. In order for any of us to understand our depression, we need to consider the traumatic wartime and postwar circumstances that brought it on. One major focal point is that we felt helpless as a result of continuing to live in an apathetic environment.

During our long months in the war zone, we found little support from Americans back home. We seemed unable to "gain any ground" in our combat situations and constantly awaited attack from our elusive enemy. It seemed that no matter how much blood, sweat, work, and death we expended, the outcome was always the same. We felt helpless.

Returning home only made matters worse because we had to avoid being identified as Nam vets, for fear of being persecuted by the citizens of our country. We were still helpless, and most of us succumbed to that sense of hopelessness. We found ourselves shrugging and saying, "Why even bother anymore?" A large number of us, myself included, took to the woods in the United States and Canada, attempting to hide out.

Depressed persons generally have a self-esteem problem. They have developed a negative self-image, often accompanied by feelings of guilt, shame, and self-criticism. Benny, a veteran of the First Infantry Division, suffers from this low self-esteem. He finds it impossible to receive a compliment of any kind. He doesn't know how to react to it and begins to stutter uncontrollably when simply trying to say thank you. He feels unworthy of any praise because of a combat incident which occurred while he was in Nam.

A gunner on a machine-gun team, Benny was assigned to conduct an ambush near a village full of women and children. Setting up at the small crossroads of a trail net-work, he and his team settled down in the humid darkness to await passing enemy troops. Something went haywire. The ambush was sprung prematurely, and Benny was re-sponsible for killing many innocent women and children in the nearby village. His stuttering today is strangely simi-lar to the incessant rattling of the M-60 machine gun he used that night.

Benny's stutter "covers" his inability to receive atten-tion others may give him in a conversation. When caught off guard, his stuttering is worse, and an intense sense of panic surrounds his attempt to defend himself. Being caught off guard is an insignificant thing for most people; they wouldn't be overly concerned about it. But to Benny, as simple a thing as having someone attempt to initiate a con-versation with him when he isn't prepared for it, can set him off. His low self-esteem and self-worth, resulting from his depressed memories from that wartime experience, have caused him to reject even the slightest compliment from others. When other people initiate conversation with Benny, he regards it as a compliment, and he simply loses it be-cause he feels unworthy of all that attention. To set up his defense perimeter, he does what he was taught to do best: lay down a good base of fire to distract and suppress what is incoming. He does this by rapidly stuttering his words.

WE WERE THE BEST ... BUT WE LOST

Vietnam was the first war America lost, and the veter-ans who fought there have lived with that reality since the war ended. It was a conflict in which we won all the battles but didn't win the war. We were the best-trained, best-equipped, biggest, and best-conditioned soldiers that America has ever put on a battlefield . . . and we knew it.

We had high-tech, computerized weapons systems. We could call in artillery or offshore bombardments anywhere we were. We had helicopters that could put us anywhere and extract us in the same manner. By all rights, we were in the "safest" war in history. One sniper round would bring the terrifying power of the modern war-machine into action. Millions of dollars in bombs and ammunition could be expended on one sniper, in one tree, in a matter of minutes. The War couldn't be lost with all that support . . . and we knew it.

We went to Vietnam under this "we know it all" delusion, and it was in our minds as we fought. It set us up for a form of depression that could never have been experienced in World War II and could be experienced only partially in Korea (because that war resulted in a stalemate). We killed nearly two million enemy Vietnamese (compared to our fifty-eight thousand dead), and throughout the conflict, we could see that more of them were dying than we were. When the war ended and we conceded victory to them, a blanket of confusion and helplessness came over every veteran who had survived and had known we were winning. The reality of defeat and the waste of so many human lives—both the dead and the "walking dead" who are with us today—was the coup de grace that sank many of us into the deep state of depression in which we live today.

We had built our lives around something that we thought was infallible, all-protecting, and unbeatable; we had believed in the indestructibility of the US military. We found out that it was fallible, poorly managed, and ultimately inferior even to a third-world army such as the Viet Cong. To top it off, we were sprayed with poison defoliants and not allowed to fight to win. When the war ended in

1975, we had to leave many of our brothers-in-arms as prisoners. Our country now claims they don't exist.

We put our faith in something that we thought was permanently strong, and we became insecure when we discovered the truth. We found out that this country, like everything else in the world, is very temporary. We made the mistake of thinking our country could keep us from evil. Neither man nor a nation of men has the power to do that.

We won every major battle, but still lost the war. It defies logic. And I believe the Communists also beat us at home by turning the press, our peers, many churches, and other antiwar sympathizers against us. We had believed, at least part of the time, that Americans were behind us.

The high-ranking officials of the Communist Vietnamese who fought against us claim that the Tet Offensive was their largest victory of the war, even though we snuffed out their intended takeover and slaughtered thousands of their troops. They say that while we busied ourselves killing their troops in Asia, the American media were reporting the slaughter to the American public. As a result, the American people resented the war even more, and the reports heightened their angry sentiments against returning soldiers.

Picture a young man who plays on a high-school football team. The team has an away game and beats the other team so severely that the young man's hometown decides his team played with too much intensity. When he gets off the bus, knowing he has performed well, his own townspeople take away his uniform and run him out of town. The result: helpless defeat and depression. This is a bit like what happened to the young men returning from Vietnam. We wanted to fight back, but we knew we couldn't take on the whole town. So we went into hiding, denying that we ever played on the team, carrying around a lot of grudges, anger, and shame we didn't dare tell anyone about. Our depression is the result of "stuffing" these incidents and of feeling that there is no path out of the maze.

We are holding on to much unexpressed resentment for things we did during the war and for sins others have accused us of doing. If anyone is wrongly blamed for a long enough period, he will begin to believe he is legitimately guilty. The resulting depression can immobilize him. Listen to one vet's confession:

> Most of the time I feel down. Since I was a kid in Nam I've been depressed. Sometimes I get so depressed that I can't even leave my bedroom. And other times I just find a dark corner in my attic and let the mental pictures of jungles, explosions, and gooks reel off like a frightening movie. Most of the time I get drunk and don't stop drinking when these times come on me. I used to sit with a pistol in my lap thinking about killing myself, but after realizing that I was so depressed that I couldn't even commit suicide, I got even more depressed and hated myself for the coward that I've turned into since coming home. Besides, I keep thinking about wiping Donovan's brains off the front of my shirt when he did himself in in a bunker at An Khe in '68. I'm home now, and I worked too hard to get here by surviving my year in Nam. I gotta live, but I ain't found much reason to in the past eighteen years.

When we came home, we got caught in a cultural crossfire. The people who opposed the war subjected us to a heavy barrage of criticism and humiliation. The "patriotic" element of society held us responsible for losing the war. We became America's scapegoat on which our country laid its sins, frustrations, and war pains so it could wipe its hands clean of any responsibility for our collective social, political, and military involvement in Vietnam. As young people, we found ourselves caught in the turmoil of this undeclared civil war, and we were the epicenter of national unrest. So we withdrew into a state of shame and denial, mixed with spiritual trauma and distrust.

Most of us found ourselves unable to compete in the job market. Many of us had dropped out of high school to serve in the war and were inadequately trained to land a skilled job. We became frustrated, unable to fit into the society that we loved and for which we had fought. Depression moved in. The vast majority of Vietnam combat veterans have been depressed since the war. And statistics tell us that each of us will significantly influence and affect a minimum of five other people in our lifetime. The potential impact upon this nation is staggering.

Help Yourself to a New Life

When you know where to find the roots of a problem, then you can deal with the problem itself. Understanding what perpetuates our problem with depression works this way. Imagine owning a car and not having the slightest mechanical inclination. One day it stalls in a busy intersection, and so you push it off to the side of the street. You open the hood because someone told you that's where you look when the engine dies. You stare dumbfounded at all that stuff under there and don't know where to begin checking for the source of your problem.

How we deal with our experiences from Vietnam and afterward is much like that. Few of us are clinicians who have treated emotional problems. Instead, we begin to short-circuit in certain areas of life, becoming anxious, depressed, seemingly out of control. Then someone says, "Look under the hood," and for the first time in our lives we admit to ourselves there may have been something from our experiences in Southeast Asia which is causing the problems in our lives.

So we "lift the hood"—that is, we begin to read or inquire about PTSD and the aftereffects of Vietnam. We are suddenly confronted with this gigantic thing called post-traumatic stress disorder, and we have absolutely no idea where to start looking for our personal problem.

As we read the VA pamphlets describing all the PTSD symptoms, we may think to ourselves, "I have them all," and may grow a bit apathetic because the problem seems overwhelming. In order to prevent being buried in all the psychological rhetoric, we who have no background in that field of study should approach our past, and the resulting problems, a step at a time and with practical, layman's methods.

Well, suppose you are standing there looking under your hood, scratching your head, and a friend comes by who has a little more knowledge about cars than you do. He says, "There are some key things you should always begin to look for when there is a problem under the hood, such as checking the electrical; maybe it's not getting any juice."

This is the same way we begin to view PTSD. We narrow down the list to a few of the obvious symptoms and take one at a time, becoming familiar with it. By looking at the major symptoms and how they make us react to life, we can then begin to identify ourselves with them. When we release ourselves from the bondage of denial and confront the fact that we exhibit some of these symptoms, we have taken the first step in becoming our own troubleshooters in dealing with PTSD.

Let me relate something personal to you. It's a little story about the time I first realized I had a problem unlike any problem normal people have. I was going through the checkout line at a grocery store one day, buying a carton of cigarettes. The line was long, and I was feeling pretty gnarly. I'd left my car running and was already late for my next stop. When I finally got to the cashier, I wrote her a check. When she asked me for an ID, I blew up and began to harass her for doubting my honesty. I slammed the cigarettes down onto the counter and stormed out. By the time I reached my car, I was trembling so much I couldn't drive. So I just sat behind the wheel and cried.

A feeling of defeat came over me. I hadn't felt like that in a long time. And then I remembered a time in Vietnam when a couple of guys got killed on our base camp perimeter. They had gone down to the dump in a Jeep to get some charcoal for a barbeque—and got ambushed! Here we were in base camp, where nothing ever happens, and the sarge and one of my best buddies got blown away, looking for charcoal so we could have a cookout! I sat on an ammo box and felt so defeated I couldn't even cry. I felt that only my skeleton prevented me from slipping off and becoming a puddle of useless, meaningless meat. The heat beat down on me like an iron fist, and my stomach was groaning with diarrhea pains. The jungle rot and heat rash on my crotch itched, and now two dudes get wasted down at the garbage dump—probably by *Mamasan*, to whom we had just given a bunch of food.

Sitting in my car at the grocery store, I realized that I hadn't trusted anyone since that incident. And here I was resenting a checkout clerk whom I thought didn't trust me. I had a tough time looking the truth in the eye, but when I did, I saw that I wasn't like the other people around me. I saw that they laughed and joked about things that I couldn't find at all humorous. I took seriously things others didn't, and I took lightly things others held up as sacred cows.

That realization was enough to pull me back into the it-don't-mean-nothin' attitude that we held on to so dearly in Nam, to save what sanity we thought we had left.

Before this event, I had thought Vietnam veterans who complained about stress and all that stuff were just conjuring up ways to get money from the government. I felt they were looking for a handout and thought this country owed them something. (As a side note, I do believe this country owes the maximum to all its veterans who have sacrificed their lives for those who didn't or wouldn't participate.) It took my experience in the grocery store in hometown America to get me to realize that I was still burdened by something from my past, something that none of these people had ever experienced. When I finally admitted that my "something" was Vietnam, I embarked on the road to recovery from those old memories that hurt so much and made me into the angry, nervous, depressed-yet-driven man I had become over the years.

PTSD covers an expansive area in our lives, and just as when we "looked under the hood" and our knowledgeable friend advised us to check out a few basic areas to locate the sources of trouble, we must view the basic symptoms of PTSD. After we've had our look, we need to honestly identify ourselves with those symptoms, or pass over them if they don't pertain to us.

The Steps to Recovery

Here are three steps you can take toward alleviating the depression you feel:

1. When a person experiences a bad incident or trauma, two emotional responses follow as a result of the shock: first, confusion, immobilization,

and disorientation with his environment; and second, denial that the incident ever took place. Currently, over 30 percent of all the men who fought in Southeast Asia will deny they were ever there. The percentage of men who admit they took part but deny they were affected is still higher. One of the most important steps to recovering from the symptom of depression is honesty with the matter. You can begin by admitting to yourself that you were in Vietnam and that there is a chance that the war has something to do with the condition you're in. You will experience considerable relief by making this simple admission.

2. If you've been depressed by a feeling of failure, for example, the best thing you can do is to find something—anything—that you can accomplish and succeed at. I know this is tough, because to tell a depressed person to do anything is applying pressure right where the hurt is. And to ask him to use personal initiative is asking him to move mountains. Nevertheless, you have to do it in order to come out from under the cloud-cover of depression. I challenge you to set a goal to get something done (no matter how trivial it may seem), and go for it. After you have done that, set another goal and then accomplish it. The key to this step is to make each goal a little more expansive or meaningful than the last.

3. As with any uncommunicated burden we carry in our minds and hearts, the best cure for this struggle within us is to talk to someone else about it. We Vietnam veterans have a special "brotherhood" that is unique in that we have difficulty in sharing our

war experiences with someone who wasn't there. I have found that revealing is healing, and the more I can tell a "brother" about my hard times, the better I feel. I encourage you to team up with another Nam brother and bare your heart to him. The final part is to go out and find someone who is in worse condition than you are and comfort or help him.

To accomplish something is your key to recovery from depression. Then, by sharing your past and opening it up to a "brother," you'll find yourself lifted higher than you could have ever imagined.

Don't give up. Everything in this world is changing; nothing stands still. If you look over the last twenty years and recognize the positive changes in society's attitude toward us as Vietnam veterans, then you can move your feelings of rejection toward those of acceptance. Memorials are being established all over the country. Being remembered through war memorials, parades, slogans, and other "welcome home" gestures bring us more hope than we've ever had since before the war. If we hang in there long enough, this life will finally pay off.

Things are changing. By firmly committing ourselves to not giving up and to enjoying our families, our work, our leisure, and our learning, we will be rewarded. The futility of a bleak future, which once surrounded us, is beginning to break, and there is something good happening. It may take a while for it all to come to pass, but it will come.

Something is there for you, so don't give up.

CHAPTER 6

Nightmares

★ ★ ★

I COULD FEEL THE DARKNESS engulf my body, my will, and the very core of my spirit. The unbearable jungle heat wrapped around me and clung like a cellophane bag. I couldn't move; to move meant giving away my position, and "Charlie" was nearby because I could smell the fish on his breath. The dark was black; I couldn't see anything. The sweat pouring from my body was the only thing moving in the whole world.

What was that? Something close! Breathing! Yes, breathing, and it's on my face. It's time to go for it—it's him or me. Like a striking snake, both my hands shot straight out and clasped the scrawny, pathetic neck in front of me, and I felt a gurgling deep in his throat as I applied pressure. I began to scream, "I'll kill you, I'll kill you!"

Suddenly, with a jerk, my prey wrenched free and was gone. The light came on, and I awoke to see my terror-stricken wife

standing at our bedroom door gasping for air as she rubbed her throat where my hands had been seconds before.
                                        —A night with a Vietnam vet

Many Vietnam veterans stay awake as long as they possibly can. For them, sleep means another night back in combat . . . preparing for a night ambush . . . lying in a hot jungle until daybreak . . . living every hour of darkness in complete terror of the unknown tactics of an elusive enemy.

So what do you do? You watch late TV, you drink jugs of coffee, you take pills—anything but fall asleep during the darkness. If you're going to go to sleep, make sure the sun is up first.

Sleep disturbance is a common plight of the Vietnam veteran. Our nightmares usually center around a feeling of helplessness or some nameless threat. Running out of ammunition while still heavily engaged with enemy forces. Being overrun by hordes of black pajamas. Stepping into a trap.

I met a widow recently who told me this sad story about her Vietnam veteran husband:

He hardly ever slept. He drank coffee continuously, and took other things to keep himself from closing his eyes. How he lasted so long without sleep is beyond me. He was afraid to sleep because he would have horrible dreams about the war, but he would never tell me about them. He would just walk around like a zombie for days after having one of these nightmares. Staying awake was his only way to protect himself.

Last year, while on a trip away from home, he died in a motel. He died in his sleep. The autopsy showed nothing unusual, but the doctor's report stated he had died of fright. He died from a bad dream.

In order to prevent sleep, or postpone it, we often use artificial stimulants to stay awake. When it becomes necessary to sleep, we use alcohol or drugs to self-medicate ourselves into a state of unconsciousness. The dangers of this lifestyle are obvious.

The seriousness of our problem with sleep disorder is that it brings about a multitude of other PTSD symptoms, simply because our bodies and mental faculties are weakened and exhausted from fear, worry, and anxiety. In other words, when we lose our built-in ability to self-restore through sleep, then we become wide-open to poor attitudes, rage, suicide (to rest at last), and depression. Another serious consequence of inability to find relief from sleep disturbance is having a nervous breakdown. Our bodies are sending us a simple message; if a major disturbance is left unchecked for too long, something is going to break.

Dread at Night, Fatigue by Day

Going to bed, or getting ready to, can bring about a heavy feeling of dread in us. It's not much different from the feeling we used to get when we knew it was our night to go on patrol. The unpleasantness of the rain, the heat, and the environment, coupled with the threat of someone waiting in ambush to kill us, frequently comes back in the form of dreams. Once sleep comes, we reexperience the death of a friend, a near capture, the fear of being overrun, the bodies being torn apart. Anyone would dream a dream like the following one:

> The midday siesta time had most of the Vietnamese down for another hour, but the bar owner in this particular village was more enterprising than the rest. He was up and around because GIs were up and around. There was money to be made.

A soldier by the name of Davis had just emerged from the "graveyard," the local opium den his unit hung out at. Whenever they were in from busy duty, their first stop was the ramshackle old hut in the middle of a gook cemetery. "Getting your head right" after being submerged in a toilet for weeks was the mandatory procedure.

Relaxing in a dilapidated bamboo chair, back in the village, Davis raised a bottle of Coke to his mouth to swig away the cotton feeling which was stuck in his throat from the drug. What at first was an ordinary glass bottle became a giant funnel as he tipped it back. He struggled, but he couldn't pull it away from his lips. His heart began to race as fear of the unknown set in, and the bottle became an awesome burden to hold. Finally, he let go of it, and it crashed to the ground. He watched it roll into the street, where it attracted all the kids in the village.

Pointing their fingers at him, they all jabbered accusingly at the wrong he had done. They completely surrounded him and began to push themselves en masse against his chair, nearly knocking it over. They were like a wave of locusts, jabbing and chewing their way into his soul.

Just as they were going to wash him away and cleanse their world of such filth, they stopped. The group parted, and a cadre of North Vietnamese soldiers marched up and took him, binding him as their prisoner.

As they got him into the street, a garbage truck pulled up, and Davis was lifted over the heads of the mob and tossed in the back. Buried in gook garbage, he swam gasping to the top of the stinking heap, to be pushed under again by one of his captors. A swirling gray and red liquid poured over him as he tried to breathe in the foul confusion.

Not all of these nightmares are full of gory combat scenes, losing loved ones, or hysterical confusion. I've had dreams about being back in the army and receiving orders to return to Vietnam. These dreams upset my whole next day, and believe me, this kind of dream is more common than experts acknowledge.

Even though it disturbs your rest, sleep disturbance has its most harmful effects during waking hours. Nightmares, whether or not you have been in combat, leave lasting impressions throughout the next day. Many people have reported terrible headaches as a result of a dream the prior night. And nightmares tend to seem inconclusive, unresolved. We sense they aren't really "over" and subconsciously work throughout the day to bring about a positive resolution. As you can easily imagine, the repercussions of having a terrible dream every time you close your eyes could be overwhelming. It makes both night and day an unreal world of brooding terrors ready to strike.

A nasty side effect is that wives of Vietnam veterans also suffer from their husbands' sleep disturbances. Some complain about being frightened as their men shout out commands and cries of terror while asleep. A more serious fear is of actual bodily harm. The wife doesn't know when her dreaming husband may be "triggered" into a combat mode that might threaten her life. The consequence is that she too begins to practice hypervigilance, losing sleep out of dread that he may hurt or kill her.

A Mixed-Up "Time Path"

Tension and anxiety are usually the result of unfounded fears. Those fears may be very real, but they are misplaced mental images on our time path. Everyone has a mental recording of everything he or she has ever experienced. On this "time path," we have real, unimagined fears of our near-death, near-pain situations in Vietnam many years ago.

These situations return to the present in the form of nightmares, complete with the scenery and events as we saw them or felt about them.

All of us attempt to sort through all the stuff on our mental record and make sense of our lives. And we all find that certain events, feelings, and situations stand out as high-impact—they shape our attitudes, feelings, and the way we see and react to life. For example, many of us view life differently than we did before we watched the assassination of John F. Kennedy on television in late November of 1963.

As veterans, the only thing abnormal about our nightmares and present sleep-disturbing thoughts is that the events on which they are based happened over thirty years ago. Our "time path" is out of order, so that when we relax and let our minds go, the trauma images of near loss of life and limb become so great, they reel off as if the events were taking place in the present.

To Sleep Is to Give Up Control

It's tough to sleep. When we go to sleep, we lose control. I don't mean that we go wild or crazy but that we are no longer in charge of our "area." We find ourselves vulnerable to outside forces, which come in the form of mental images. The feelings and thoughts we associate with these images disturb and interrupt our rest.

Most of the time, our mental pictures are recurring; they are the same each time. As with any traumatic experience, these images are lodged in portions of our mind we simply can't control. That's why few humans, if any, can remember all the things that pass through their minds while they sleep. This section of the mind acts like a shock absorber or circuit breaker. When the load gets too heavy for our conscious mind, it shuts off, and everything begins to react automatically through this "mysterious" sector. Consequently, we remember little of the full content in these dream images but enough that it has an adverse affect on our lives.

We are vulnerable while we sleep. That's why many of us stay awake as long as we possibly can. Awake equals control; sleep equals no control. The irony is that by trying to keep control of the night (staying awake), we begin to lose control of our waking world. Our bodies were made to recuperate through rest.

Since dreams have a way of discharging mental energy, they become "work" for many of us veterans. We wake up feeling exhausted instead of resting. But, I believe there are ways to break this cycle.

THE STEPS TO RECOVERY

Here are three steps you can take toward recovery from sleep disturbance and nightmares:

1. Do not hesitate to seek professional medical help. Go to a doctor who can evaluate your condition and give you competent, professional suggestions. In some cases, medication may be necessary to help you "cool down" (or rest up) before you try anything else.

2. Recognize that your mental and physical time paths don't coincide. One of the best things you can do is to talk about the present with someone else. A sensitive person can help you see and accept that you are probably not in any present danger. You need to begin to make clear distinctions between past experience and present reality. Then you'll have to train yourself to argue against the seeming "immediacy" of your war traumas, brought on by feelings and thoughts with ones based on truth and

present reality. "Talking about it" will also serve to diffuse the "hot" areas that have gripped your attention and held it for all these years. You've got to get to the root cause of your problem and dump it once and for all. Revealing is healing. By talking about your dreams and nightmares with another Vietnam veteran, you'll begin to break the binding influence they have over you.

3. Be persistent. Don't stop talking until you find relief. You'll have to keep working through your time path until you get to the incident or incidents which have got you blocked. You'll know when you find the root cause because you'll sense a wave of relief, and the symptoms of sleep disturbance will come to an end. Sometimes it goes away abruptly, other times gradually. Keep on it until you "dust off" the thing for good.

CHAPTER 7

Survival Guilt and "Things I've Done"

★ ★ ★

WE SPENT THREE WEEKS *at Bien Hoa Airbase completely iso-lated from outsiders. We ate nothing but "gook food," so that our sweat would smell like the natives. We turned in our army gear, and they issued us Chinese and Russian weapons, black pajamas, sandals, and "rice paddy hats." During the night, we would slip out of our tiny compound and probe Ameri-can perimeter lines. This was to accustom us to being on the other side. I actually felt more secure "out there" than I ever did when I was assigned to an American unit.*

During that same time we would receive "special" instruc-tions about our new war. We learned stuff that not even the top brass in Vietnam would ever get their hands on.

I'll never forget our first "pacification" mission. Two of us (Americans) were assigned to a five-man friendly gook team and dropped off under cover of darkness near a small village somewhere north of the Iron Triangle. It was around two in the morning when we entered the village, and the friendly gooks rousted out a family into the center of the hooches. Three small children, one in a mother's arms, an old lady, and old man. The entire family was quickly beaten to the ground, shot through the head, and disemboweled by our counterparts. I held back my vomit, as I retched deeply in the guts. My American partner and I hung back as lookouts, so we wouldn't be identified as Americans by the rest of the villagers. Upon leaving the village, the friendlies yelled out obscenities to the rest of the village, and made verbal evidence that we were Viet Cong.

The purpose of the mission was to win the "hearts, souls, and minds" of the people by letting them know just how bad the Viet Cong were, when really it was us trying to make them look bad. The mentality of that war was absolutely unreal, and I'll never be able to forgive myself for allowing that to happen.

—A teenage Phoenix operative on his
second tour in Vietnam

Operations in Vietnam, such as the infamous Phoenix Program, serve as evidence that Vietnam was a different kind of war, bringing with it a new face to the subject of guilt. MAAG, Phoenix, and Special Operations Group (SOG) were some of the most common CIA operations carried on during the war. They not only operated in Vietnam, but also conducted many "sterile" missions into Laos and Cambodia. "Sterile" meant that the team would go into action completely stripped of any identification that would link them to the US, South Vietnam, or any other country. If captured, the troops were on their own and would not be claimed by any government.

In any war, a God-fearing and people-respecting person would naturally feel guilt at taking another life. The reality of "honorable killing," such as killing an enemy soldier with the intent of preserving freedom and justice, alleviates much of that guilt because the action is blessed by a grateful and agreeing nation. A Vietnam veteran who was involved in special operations, such as "Phoenix," carries an awesome burden of guilt. Some attempted to escape through anonymity, as you can see in the following testimonial of a US Army Lt. Colonel:

> I was given a name and a place to report to, and suddenly I discovered that I was right back in Special Forces. They asked me to become a part of the Phoenix Program, a CIA-run operation whose basic purpose was to identify Viet Cong and eliminate them. The first thing I learned about the operation was that although it amounted to political assassination, they called it "execution" because, I suppose, it gave the whole thing a more judicious ring, a sort of legal mantle. What they wanted me to do was to take charge of execution teams that wiped out entire families and tried to make it appear as though the VC themselves had done the killing. . . . I agreed to some kind of mission or assignment but not that . . . I saw guys I'd known in Special Forces back at Fort Bragg, North Carolina, whose names were entirely different in Vietnam. Maybe that was one way of escaping any guilt feelings about their work.

Many Americans participated in this Phoenix Program. Today, they continue to punish themselves for things they did and things they could have prevented—actions connected with this supersensitive, top-secret program to win the Vietnam War. It's a guilt which they can't talk about for fear the CIA will reenter their lives—this time to eliminate them.

The number of people who served in special operations and witnessed clandestine atrocities is greater than most people think. We don't hear about them because these men are not at liberty to talk. In fact, they can't even participate in the usual rap group sessions the VA offers for Vietnam veterans, because the government is afraid that "sensitive" information may leak out, compromising the CIA and the US government.

"Why Wasn't It Me Instead?"

But what about the "normal" soldier in Vietnam? Our typical tour did not encompass such unique adventures as Phoenix and SOG. Still, the guilt of veterans involved in the "normal" war does have peculiarities of its own. What characterizes our guilt?

As I stated earlier, the Vietnam War produced more survivors than any other war in our country's history. Only 58,044 died. Because of the high-tech medical practices and the speedy evacuation by helicopter, a wounded man who would have died under the conditions found in World War II or the Korean War, most likely lived through Vietnam. This has resulted in the most predominant form of guilt in Vietnam vets: survivor guilt.

1. "Why did I live when other people died?"
2. "I should have died, and they should have lived."
3. "It should have been me instead."

These are expressions of survivor guilt. As survivors, we tend to want to trade places with the person who died. Time and again, I've heard veterans say that the guys who died were the lucky ones, because they don't have to be around to suffer the pain and agony of shame, unemployment, Agent Orange poisoning, flashbacks, depression, and nightmares.

We go through wide and varying mood swings with this type of guilt. We may have excessive anxiety and tension, sleep problems, and flashbacks that are tripped off by our environment. We can experience severe self-doubt and set out to punish ourselves for surviving when others more "worthy" died during the war.

As survivors, we can go from being quite normal, to a low state of depression, then swing into a high state of hyperalertness and anxiety in a matter of minutes. Especially if our life situation becomes tumultuous. Tensions in our daily life, such as marital problems, employment difficulties, poor health, and financial worries, can trigger our stressors to turn on.

Those of us who have high-stress, highly active occupations are the most vulnerable to the symptoms of survivor guilt. Our environment impinges into our thoughts so much that flashbacks occur regularly. We tend to seek out stimulants or depressants (drugs and alcohol) to keep ourselves together. This can become a major and dangerous problem to overcome. Many superactive war survivors use adrenaline for medication. Many take high risks in occupations or recreational sports, such as rock climbing, parachuting, or racing cars and motorcycles. Some of us find exciting relief through torrential sexual encounters with many partners.

As you can easily imagine, living with a Vietnam veteran who suffers from survivor guilt can be a harrowing experience. It's not easy trying to keep up with someone who is running fast enough to blot out his mental images of a past time of terror, pain, and a feeling of unworthiness. It's a job in itself trying to pin us down long enough to attempt giving us some help.

THE IMPULSE TO SELF-DESTRUCT

Many of us who suffer from survivor guilt lead interesting "flashpan" lives. By that I mean that we travel precarious paths and seem to look for the biggest guy in the bar to fight, knowing full well we'll probably get our brains beat out. But we go at him anyway. Some of us feel we have to give all the time and lead lives of propitiation. Some men become compulsive blood donors and seem to find considerable relief in giving their blood so others can live.

The number of single-car accidents among Vietnam veterans is staggering. Even though we will never claim to be suicidal, the most guilt-ridden of us seem to find ways of destroying ourselves—whether it be taking on the whole Hell's Angels motorcycle club in a barroom brawl, a shoot-out with a SWAT team, or a reckless ingestion of drugs and alcohol in the disguise of seeking fun.

ALL USED UP

Guilt is an emotional disturbance resulting from behavior commonly agreed upon as wrong. Breaking a law or an agreement can send this emotional disturbance into action. Some indicators of guilt are depression, self-punishment, low self-esteem, headaches, chronic fatigue, constant criticism of others, and fear of setting out on new tasks because you think you're incompetent or a failure.

Many of us went to Vietnam trained to kill the enemy. But few of us were mentally prepared for the reality of that action and its ensuing consequences. I don't remember ever being trained to psychologically withstand the shock of losing a close friend or maybe one of my limbs. At times, I feel the military expected us to some how walk through the fire without getting burned. It didn't work out that way, though, and now the government seems to be scratching its head, wondering what to do about us.

If guilt is left unattended, a change begins to occur. The veteran gets "used up" by it and becomes lethargic about life. It may take considerable push to get him to move freely on his own initiative.

When a person has guilt, he also begins to lose his creative energy. One of the most devastating events that can take place is for someone to openly accuse him of doing something wrong. Shame brings his guilt out into the light, and the slightest public accusation can trigger a number of antisocial behaviors and PTSD symptoms.

Like a heavily laden backpack, guilt can sap us of life's vitality.

"I Was Stationed Elsewhere" Guilt

Guilt from surviving when others did not is one of the heaviest loads a veteran can carry. To spend years of silent confusion, wondering why "he got it and I didn't" is common in many Nam vets. But there is another guilt that can be equally devastating—a form many take lightly. Guilt from not having "been there" at all.

I've found that many navy personnel who were stationed offshore during the Vietnam War have tremendous feelings of guilt. Support troops stationed in secure areas such as Saigon, Thailand, Okinawa, Guam, and the Philippines also are burdened with guilt because their wartime roles kept them in relatively comfortable and safe surroundings. In fact, most of these people don't even consider themselves Vietnam veterans.

This I-wasn't-there guilt can cause extensive problems with low self-esteem. It becomes quite apparent when these support veterans associate with combat veterans. Even the troops who served in Korea and Germany and other non-combat theaters during the Vietnam era carry a load of guilt for not being in the action. The truth is that someone had to be where they were stationed to do those jobs, and they happened to be the ones who got chosen.

MEDICAL PERSONNEL AND GUILT

Medical personnel who were sent into combat to patch up the wounded and to save lives on the battlefield often suffer the most painful symptoms of guilt. These people were trained for a few months and sent to a unit to become the "Doc." With a limited amount of medical knowledge, these people performed courageously and saved many lives. Some of the troops they tried to save, however, didn't make it. Many of these wounded were beyond all medical help and died much to the dismay of the medic attending them. Consequently, the medic harbors a lot of pain because of his inability or "incompetence" to have saved the soldier's life. For these brave men who did their best with what they had, the hurtful memories linger to this day. They still blame themselves for others' deaths.

Other medical personnel admit guilt because they developed an intense hatred for the Vietnamese people. Since it was difficult to identify the enemy, nobody, including the medical people, knew who to blame for all the terrible wounds they witnessed daily. So all Asians became their targets. When they had to work on wounded Vietnamese, in many cases they treated them roughly and abusively. Today, these medics live with the guilt of having had these horrible feelings against the very people they were sent to defend.

Since female nurses were not allowed to accompany combat units into the field, their form of survivor guilt comes from a different source. First, they feel guilty because they never had to suffer the hardships of "humping" the boonies and living in jungle and rice-paddy war conditions. Secondly, they feel guilty because they could not do more to save lives from where they were stationed.

Sometimes the lack of medical supplies posed problems. But the major reality was the fact that men, who should have been killed, were brought back for them to attend. They saw men who would have died in previous wars, live and suffer on their operating tables. Men with severe amputations, burns, and multiple fragment wounds lived to tell these nurses about the horrors of the battle. In the past wars, men so torn up would have been quickly stuffed into body bags and sent home. The medical personnel never would have seen them. But in Vietnam there was row after row of walking dead.

I have a special friend who served as a nurse at the 93d Field Evacuation Hospital at Long Binh. She was one of the nurses who patched up my unit after it nearly got wiped out on Hill 875 at Dak To. Our own planes dropped napalm on the 173d Airborne by mistake while it was engaged in heavy fighting to take the hill. (In fact, the scene in the movie *Platoon*, in which the troops get bombed with napalm, was a take-off on this particular battle.)

During the course of the action and confusion, she had the ghastly job of tending the young paratroopers who had survived. They brought the wounded down in helicopters and the dead in dump trucks, dumping them off at Pleiku like garbage. My nurse friend tells me there was one thing about the whole episode that sticks in her mind. In her words, "All the bodies were already rotting . . . the dead and the living."

To have witnessed this tragedy has caused her inexpressible grief, heartache, and guilt. Fortunately, she has found a way and some good friends to help her recover from most of her war-caused problems.

THE STEPS TO RECOVERY

While I-wasn't-there guilt is usually built on hypothetical realities or imagined problems, survivor guilt is based on the harshest of truths: the actual death of someone close enough that it could have happened to either the victim or the survivor. There are three steps you can take that will help you find relief from survivor's guilt:

1. Your recovery from the guilt caused by surviving when someone else did not begins when you can separate out the responsibilities in the incident. Force yourself to think it through. Face your grief squarely and separate what is rational, logical, or cognitive from that which is simply emotional— and sometimes imagined. You may have to actually list the facts about certain incidents on paper or write out your experiences in order to determine what you actually believe about them. Once you see what is true about each situation, according to the facts, you will begin to view your inappropriate emotion of guilt or grief as something that needs to be dealt with. Often you will recognize that the death of someone else had very little to do with whether you remained alive or died with him. This task of sorting out can bring you to the point of taking responsibility for your past (and present) actions, while at the same time allowing you to freely feel emotions of sadness, anguish, and grief as part of the healing process.

2. The second simple release from this form of guilt is to know that it's OK to feel sad about the person who died in the incident. But it is equally important to know that dwelling on it doesn't help. Some memories come to us of their own accord. You don't have to compound your problem by dredging up others in order to feel as miserable as you think you should.

3. The third release you can give yourself is to realize that the enemy killed your friend or friends in battle, and your survival doesn't mean you had anything to do with their deaths. If you have to blame something for killing your friends, blame the war, not yourself.

Perhaps the most important resource you can use to bind up these wounds and begin to heal them is to seek out another Vietnam veteran and unload the entire incident on him. Keep unloading. It is very important to tell the whole story, not just parts of it. Tell as many details as possible. Remembering smells, noises, the type of clothing you were wearing, and other environmental conditions can guide you into a more precise recollection. Going over your story many times will help you remember more things, and as you tell it again and again, you'll find growing confidence to open up and tell more.

Recognize that you will probably experience sudden bursts of grief during these story-telling times. It's OK to let it all go. Nobody has ever died from crying. Once you get it out, you'll feel much better. When you've detailed your entire story to a listening and understanding "brother," you'll find your healing process to be remarkably rapid.

Dealing with I-wasn't-there guilt is quite similar and straightforward. I've found that much healing occurs when a support vet and a combat vet finally sit down and each talk about their own versions of the war. If you have problems with this kind of guilt, here are a few tips for your conversation. Do not apologize—that's the last thing a combat veteran wants to hear. Be real and talk about your job. Be very specific about your duties.

I can tell you, that after a good friend of mine told me how hard the work had been on an aircraft carrier off the Gulf of Tonkin, I began to think that my life in War Zone D had been a piece of cake. He worked his rear off night and day to keep the ship running and those aircraft going around the clock. I listened and he talked, and then I talked and he listened. At the end, we had woven a bond that had been missing in both of our lives—a bond we didn't even know was supposed to be there.

We emerged on equal ground. He had been feeling bad because he hadn't suffered the hardships of "humping" in the war, and I had felt he had held a slack job. Now I respected him for being a hard-working man who was backing me up all the way. This kind of interaction with a combat veteran will not necessarily come easily. But if you are persistent, you will find peace with each other and your absentee guilt will subside.

CHAPTER 8

Outbursts
of Rage

★ ★ ★

I WAS WORKING AT A CHEAP electronics store. I needed money, and it was one of the many temporary jobs I had since coming back from Nam. Selling wasn't too tough for me if I didn't have to answer a lot of questions about the product. I just wanted to make some money, not become an expert on the product.

Well, one day some electronics-whiz yuppie came in to buy some worthless gadget, and he started asking every stupid question he could think of. I knew he already had the answers; he just wanted to test me out. I felt a chill hit me, and the next thing I knew I had the guy laid across the counter, yelling wildly in his face. I had to go home right then and there.

As I left, I could feel everyone looking at me, and I wanted to cry out, "Leave me alone!" I was terribly alone. I'm sure that hundreds of demons were living in my head, and it was times like this that they crept out and took control of my whole being. I don't understand, nobody else understands; but it seems

*as if I need to let a little of the pain out along the way, or I'll
explode and do something really crazy.*

—A Vietnam Veteran

Rage resulting from post-traumatic stress disorder and
the Vietnam War is a behavior that leaves many of us vets
depressed. For no apparent reason we can lash out at whom-
ever is around us when our environment begins to put stressors on us. By *stressors* I mean pressure stimulations, such
as interrogation-type conversation, being "put on the spot,"
near accidents, observing what we consider unsafe conditions, heavy-handed authoritarian tactics from associates,
instructors, law enforcement officers, and employers.

This rage reaction is usually so turbulent that it not only
frightens everyone around us, but ourselves as well. Those
who witness our outbursts think we're insane. Unfortunately, our wives, children, and closest associates get the
brunt of this horrifying behavior because of their close proximity in our day-to-day activities and relationships.

Some veterans put their fists through walls and break
things in these sudden rages. They've found that doing this
is a way to sublimate their violence, or at least to unleash it
against things instead of people. Many have discovered certain signs that tip them off to an outbreak of rage in-the-
making. When they detect it coming, they quickly leave
the scene before something or someone gets hurt. I personally had hyperalertness about my family's safety. I used to
detect my anger flaring and would immediately jump into
my car and drive like a maniac to vent my rage. This was a
very, very dangerous way to deal with it, but at that time I
wasn't in control.

I remember times when I would come home late at night
and find the front door unlocked or even slightly open. I

would fly into a rage and begin yelling to wake up everybody because of this blatant case of "lax security." I would worry excessively about unpreparedness and imagine the worst in all possible events. I would flip into a crisis state at the drop of a hat if it landed wrong. Everything had to be in order and ready for . . . I didn't know what; just ready.

A Byproduct of Our Training

So what do we, as Vietnam veterans, need to know about our rage? Anyone who has ever gone through military training will confess that he or she began to experience rage as an initial feeling toward the training cadre, the regimentation, the physical training, and mental abuse. It was our rage at these things which we had to suppress because of the penalties we would face for being discourteous to superiors.

Resentment, frustration, and helplessness are all feelings any basic training course will implant, but in peacetime these feelings melt away once the training is completed. By the time a peacetime soldier is discharged, he will move smoothly back into society with few or no residual problems from his experience.

In basic training, we were intentionally pushed to our limits to boil the killer instinct to the surface of our personalities. We were ordered and conditioned into frenzied rage in order for us to complete the task of war, which is killing other human beings. Soon we fell in and were molded to do that. One doesn't kill and look for others to kill, on a daily basis for a year, without adopting a philosophy to continue to do so. We worked ourselves into explosive machines that wouldn't stop until all was dead. It took rage to carry us through all of it. Now we react in a similar way when we get ticked off, and it comes across as overkill because we attempt to stamp out the disturbance or problem so that it never happens again. We have a terminal attitude, but most things don't require it.

We went to Vietnam harboring this suppressed rage from our training, and the war compounded the problem. After all those long weeks and months of harassment, we entered the combat in South Vietnam, where the frustrations of guerrilla warfare took their toll. The enemy was elusive. We rarely ever saw who we were fighting, but our well-concealed enemy struck us with deadly effect. We watched our friends get their legs and arms blown off by booby traps. We nearly died every day from the mortar rounds, ambushes, and snipers. We wanted to fight back, but our enemy always disappeared, leaving us with no outlet for our pent-up fury. We wanted to pay back some of the hurt that engulfed us. At the first opportunity to unleash this rage, our violent impulses would surge and we would strike out indiscriminately. Our targets were not always the proper ones.

The massacres of innocents, such as what happened at My Lai, is evidence of this. Lieutenant Calley and others involved in the My Lai incident were not the only ones who killed innocent people; they were just poorly used examples. Our need to kill something—anything that represented the enemy, Vietnam, authority, or opposition—was frequently vented explosively upon innocent bystanders.

SETTING UP AN EMOTIONAL "PERIMETER"

Many Vietnam veterans lack a natural love and compassion for others, even for their own family. This stands as glaring proof of the hard casing we have built around ourselves. We use our intense anger as a weapon to ward people off so they don't get too close.

Not long ago, I got a call from a vet friend in Washington, DC. He said his wife had left him, and he needed to talk. He then told me about how he had started having flash-backs and reactions to Vietnam after she'd left. He'd had no problems with PTSD in his twenty tears since he returned from Nam. He said that he'd been a squad leader in Nam, and his entire squadron was killed in an ambush, except for him. He had loved those guys dearly and had vowed to himself that he would never let another person get inside his heart again. His wife had made it inside his perimeter—the defense wall he had put in place to keep people at arm's length—and now she was gone. He felt exactly the way he had twenty years ago in that ambush. Fortunately, I was able to connect him with one of our "Point Men" on the East Coast, and he's finally come home.

The hard-shelled "perimeter" that most of us set up is meant to numb the emotions and outer feelings. It was a defense mechanism we put in place because of our con-stant threat of death and loss in Vietnam.

Our unspoken rationale for this self-controlled mecha-nism was that our showing feelings of sorrow, pain, or guilt opened up the "perimeter" and let others inside with us. We didn't want anyone else inside. Today, many of us still wear this shell of protection. It is a cold, numb armor of unfeeling that we wear to protect ourselves. Inside that armor, a well of tears and feelings wait to be unleashed, and quite often they break out as boiling anger against those around us. Since we can't shoot an M-16 over people's heads to keep them at bay, we fire megatons of raging abuse in their direction and let them know they'd better leave us alone.

Rage comes with frightening regularity for some veter-ans. Regardless of the regret and shame we feel afterward, we still explode with no apparent reason. I've had prob-lems in this area myself, and I can remember trying to hold myself in some kind of bondage. I would get irritable at

NAM VET: MAKING PEACE WITH YOUR PAST

first and then slowly build up to a fairly good-sized explosion. Usually, I directed it against my family, because they happened to be nearby. I always ended up feeling so bad that I would sink into a terrible depression. Time and again, I vowed to change this futile pattern of behavior—which was scaring my family half to death—only to settle into a dark despair. I felt doomed to endure this craziness forever. Since that time, however, something has changed inside of me. I'll tell you more about that later.

A Shocking Self-Discovery

Rage against oneself is fairly common among us. I believe that this inner self-hatred and self-anger is probably the most horrifying and misunderstood feeling that we have. Many of us experienced, for the first time in our lives, our true potential to commit violent acts. In our pent-up feelings of rage, we recognized the killer inside us. We were shocked to find him there, ready when needed. Our struggles to survive combat set free many emotions and actions which are too terrible to recall. We hate ourselves for having thought them or carried them into action. We want to forget these feelings because they remind us of the "bad" persons we think we really are.

Many of us hide these terrifying memories, but find ourselves flying off the handle under the stresses of daily living. A baby crying, someone slamming a door, an angry boss, or an argument with another driver during rush hour can set us off. Our sudden urge to want to destroy again, without reservation, takes a lot of energy for us to suppress. After the feeling finally subsides, we confirm to ourselves that we truly are "bad" persons. So we harbor the need to hide our feelings even better, for fear that someone else will find out how bad we really are.

STRIKING OUT AT ASIANS

It's easy to understand why veterans of a war like Vietnam would display such fits of rage against Asians here in America. The old man who sold us soda in the day would shoot at us at night. The black market and crime were so rampant among the Vietnamese during the war that we readily remember the times they tried to screw us out of something. After a while, we felt that the only reason the "friendly" Vietnamese wanted us there was so we would fight their war for them while they conned us out of our money. Without these two benefits, we believed they couldn't have cared less about us. They secretly despised us, preferring to be associated with their own . . . even if "their own" were enemy troops from up north.

This used-by-the-Vietnamese feeling, added to the antiwar sentiment we knew was burgeoning at home, dug within us a well of anger, which has grown deeper through the ensuing years. The reason it has developed to such frightening proportions is because we have never had an outlet to vent and release these feelings, nor anyone who would understand us.

Many of us who have worked with refugees now living in America find it difficult to trust them. We may experience flashbacks when we are around them and begin to feel uneasy or insecure. Before you know it, we're looking for a reason to get angry with them.

WHERE WAS GOD?

Because many of us struggle with an impaired capacity to love and care for others, we find ourselves setting up a perimeter of defense against God, too. After all, don't most people associate love and caring with a loving God? If that's the way He is, then He, too, must be shut out.

We set this survival mechanism in place because of the constant horror in the war. We felt God had skipped out in Vietnam. He went AWOL. Whatever protection we were going to get would come from our own natural means. So we cursed God and forgot Him. We replaced Him with survival skills and logic.

There are many of us who still seethe with resentment toward God. We went to Southeast Asia in good faith to fight a war. We had always believed that God would look after us, even if we didn't behave like saints, because we were fighting against atheist Communists who abhorred God. We blamed God for the horrors we saw and experienced, and for our eventual loss of the war.

We also blamed God for what we saw chaplains doing during the war. Many (though not all, for some were godly men) of God's representatives in the military had a bad habit of working on deadlines, statistics, and self-gratification. I have heard a lot of Vietnam veterans comment that the chaplains weren't there to tell them about Jesus, but to try to win soldiers over to their denominations. Every time they came around, it felt like being cornered by someone who was zealously trying to get you to join a multilevel sales organization. It would almost make you vomit. And there were other examples of this disgusting religious hypocrisy.

A vet told me about the following incident that affected his feelings about God and the men who serve Him. "One time I saw a chaplain ordering wounded soldiers off a medevac chopper in the middle of a firefight so they could make room for him to get on and out of harm's way. Where was his God?"

As you can see, we have set up a perimeter against all emotions (such as caring and loving) and against all people whom we regard as weak. The God who says turn your other cheek so your enemy can strike it, too, seemed to us to be asking the impossible, while He allowed horrible evils to engulf us and the people we cared about. We have our defenses set against the feelings we know contain our cure.

WHAT CAN YOU DO WITH THIS RAGE?

Many of us ask ourselves almost daily, "What can I do with this surging emotion inside me?" We survived long months of constant life-threatening circumstances, watched others around us get maimed and killed by an unseen enemy, and then we had no way to release our pent-up emotions and urges to "pay back" the wrongs committed against us and our friends. This frustration has become yet another unseen enemy—one that operates in our present lives.

We were conditioned to strike out against wrongs, but now we sometimes overreact to otherwise normal encounters around us. I suppose this is why many of us have thought, *I'm crazy and I hope nobody else finds out.* Many times we find ourselves pumping up extra surges of adrenaline to cope with or terminate a simple problem in our "area."

There are a number of ways we can effectively deal with this rage. Here are five suggestions which may help to tame that lion within us.

STEPS TO RECOVERY

1. Although your pent-up anger and outbursts of rage may have led you to think you are crazy, believe me that PTSD is not a mental illness. Your problems are stress-related, not a mental disease. PTSD is a stressful reaction to the conditions of war, and your first step to quelling your anger will begin when you understand and accept this fact.
2. The primary step in recovering from rage set in place by our experiences in training and in Vietnam, is one

which requires us to take a second look at an example I used earlier. A few pages back, I described how I used to come home late at night and blow my top because I found the front door unlocked. In my railing against my family for not keeping tighter security, I was dealing with something they considered completely unimportant. It never occurred to them to think of unlocked doors as a threat—not where we lived. I realized this one day, after one of my outbreaks, when I saw for the first time the innocence in their eyes. I recognized that I had a problem. I was trying to make my problem theirs, too. Identifying the triggering situation from an "innocent's" eyes is a healing touch that will perform miraculous results in defusing the rage you hold inside. Compassion is the ability to see life's situations through another's eyes. If you can step back briefly before each episode of rage sets in, and look at the situation at hand through the eyes of the person on the other side, you will be in position to maintain control. If you step back, take a deep breath, and defuse yourself with compassion, you will be able to experience peace where rage would normally have controlled you.

3. If step number two doesn't work for you, then you may need to temporarily pull out until you cool down. I find that if I can't step back and regroup when I'm tripped off by another person's "offense" or a "weird" situation, I'm better off to simply remove myself from the setting for a while. Don't misunderstand me. I'm not advocating running from the problem. What I am saying is that going somewhere and sitting down and thinking things through a little is usually good medicine. Collecting the situation and analyzing it a

little before taking action normally puts you, rather than your emotions, in control.

4. It is also OK to let your anger out on occasion. Expressing rage is highly effective in defending against depression, which is our most common PTSD symptom. It can release pent-up energy that needs to be expelled from the soul. Although the outward manifestation of it may be terrifying, getting angry and letting it out can be a healing process in itself. There are ways to do this without having to hurt people. Use some worthless inanimate object as your target. Or if your rage is directed against a specific person or group of people, imagine them sitting in the chair across from you and let them have it some night when you are home alone. Make sure you use a chair no one will miss—pick one up at a junkyard or yard sale. Or if you express your anger verbally, picture the person sitting in the chair and tell him what you think of him and what he did. While these tactics may sound silly to you, like a child pretending to talk to an invisible friend, they work. They are commonly used by therapists to help people face fears and hurts in their past.

Finally, as with all major PTSD symptoms, rage is best handled by confiding with a Nam brother who can walk down the same trail with you and "watch your back" while you heal.

CHAPTER 9

PTSD and the Veteran's Family

★ ★ ★

WE HAD NO VETERAN FRIENDS *(at least none I knew of). From what I had heard through the media . . . Vietnam veterans* were potentially dangerous men. *Explosive* time bombs *who felt sorry for themselves.*

My husband was a helicopter gunner in the 101st Airborne, 1967–1968. He was one of the ones who came home, started back to school, and went on with his life.

He advanced professionally, contributing to his field. As he approached his mid-thirties, he became more driven. He began to drink excessively, to show explosive anger, or to withdraw and "isolate" himself. His physical complaints became more numerous. He became dissatisfied with everything he was doing—professional and personal. Yet, he always said he was "just fine." He did not know what was causing it, so he could not share what he was feeling. I watched him come apart and felt helpless. Powerless to do anything.

Much of this we hid from those around us. We both lived behind our need to maintain the facade—each of us for different reasons. One face to the world, another at home. No one outside knew—not family, not friends, not business associates— no one.

To the outside world we were "fine." Yet our relationship was coming apart like the scattered pieces of a puzzle. There were good times. And when it was good . . . it was wonderful. The stress would lift and he would be humorous, up, and supportive. But much of the time he was miserably unhappy, and there was little I could do to help him or myself. I felt isolated. The hardest part was not knowing or understanding where this profound unhappiness originated.

—A Nam vet's wife
(Letter from Misha Halverson, 1986)

Vietnam veterans are not the only victims of the war. Our families likewise suffer from the effects of PTSD. The emotional numbing, depression, and alienation that have isolated the veteran from his family are symptoms of his post-traumatic stress from the war. The veteran's symptoms are usually obvious. But the psychological wounds within the family are not as readily perceived.

Research clearly indicates that families of veterans are affected both emotionally and spiritually by the veteran's stress. To help yourself you must also help your family. They need to have a deep understanding of things that cause or trigger your reactions. Certain things that would hardly bother persons who never experienced Vietnam have become your survival mechanisms. For instance:

1. *Beer or pop cans.* The majority of us always crush cans because they can easily be made into booby

traps and hand grenades. We aren't being macho when we do this; we're just practicing survival skills.

2. *Cars backfiring, or the sound of helicopters.* These noises automatically put us on the offense.

3. *Mildew.* With the constant dampness of Vietnam, everything mildewed, including our skin.

4. *The smell of urine.* A reminder of the filth and dead bodies.

5. *Rain.* When it rained in Vietnam (most of the time), the enemy came, men died, it was cold, and we couldn't see or hear what was going on, even when our lives depended on it.

We react to many situations with a startle response, which can turn an ordinary occurrence into a crisis. Many times, this reaction can manifest itself as hostility. Our wives and children, since they are usually the closest, become our prime targets for this hostility. Our families need to know the things that set us off. Give them a fair chance. Tell them.

The most difficult thing for your family members to do is to keep from taking any attack of anger or hostility as a personal affront. Often your anger and attack are directed at yourself, the government, the no-win syndrome of Vietnam, or your inability to be in control of events around you. It is frightening for a veteran's family to live with his unpredictable emotions on a daily basis. It is akin to living with an alcoholic, who lives with and for a bottle.

STUFFING IT INSIDE FOR TOO LONG

Many people think of the Nam vet as a stereotype: a guy living on the street in a field jacket, packing a big knife, drunk, drugged, and crazy. That is far from a true image.

Thousands of vets are professionals, highly paid white-collar workers, with fine families and influential friends. Even so, most of us have been "stuffing" the Vietnam experience inside for decades. Beneath our "together" exterior writhes a seething pool of uncommunicated frustration, guilt, and the worst monster of all: denial. (Many of us who married after the war, never told our spouses we had been in Nam. In 1986, it was estimated that over one-quarter of all who served in Vietnam still denied that they were veterans of the war.)

The world around us may think we have no problems, and most people would guess we were never in Nam. But many of us display little quirks around our families that give us away. We are a bit fanatical about cleanliness, order, and especially security. If we come home late and find the house unlocked, we throw a tantrum that borders on panic. Our family suffers, walking on eggshells, never knowing when we may fly off the handle completely. (Even though we've never done it, they feel we may at any time.) They live on the edge of something they can't explain.

In the meantime, our pool of uncommunicated experiences fills and fills. Eventually, we can hold no more inside, and it overflows. Our reactions, quirks, and symptoms begin to pour out, perhaps not as flagrant bursts of insanity—our friends and families may diagnose these as normal life problems—but they are definite PTSD symptoms that need to be dealt with.

Some of us never realize that PTSD is the cause of our problems. We live in a private hell. We secretly struggle to find resolution for our war experiences, and under the pressure we unwittingly use our families as the unfortunate targets of our stress.

WHAT GOES AROUND, COMES AROUND

Many children of veterans with PTSD are deprived of a carefree childhood. Real emotional closeness is difficult for many of us, and in our homes we are overprotective and overdemanding. Our children grow up afraid they will never measure up to our expectations, and we tend to emphasize achievement as the golden rule.

I attest to being instrumental in forcing my teenage daughter into maturity at a young age. I wanted her to "get an early start" on life. It boiled down to my lack of patience in living with her through what I thought were useless years of childhood. She finished high school at the age of fifteen and was into a career school at sixteen. The problem is this: we have difficulty accepting childlike behavior because we're afraid it leaves our kids too vulnerable.

When our family members see us isolating ourselves and numbing our emotions, they begin to believe that this is the way life is supposed to be lived. The wife forgets how to laugh, and our children grow up afraid of making any loud and sudden noises, which are a natural part of growing up. As a result, they begin to avoid intimate contact because they quickly learn that they invariably get hurt when they get close to someone they love.

Maybe we have never struck our wives or children in a sudden outburst of rage (many vets with PTSD have), but the very threat that we might, looms over our families and terrifies them. We can be erratic and unpredictable, bouncing from rage to remorse. This keeps our loved ones constantly on alert, dreading our often-submerged, but pervasive hostility.

STILL WEARING THE BRICK OVERCOAT

A lot of our suppressed anger is directed at ourselves. When people find they cannot control their environment, they either repress or express their frustration. Family life provides many situations where we Nam vets feel that our environment is out of control. To lose control in Vietnam usually meant that someone was going to die. When things happened to cause pain, death, and sorrow, our environment was out of our control. It was so far beyond our control that we couldn't even find an appropriate target to release our hostilities or retaliatory feelings against. Instead, we beefed up our brick overcoat of numbness and walked away from sensitive situations with an attitude of "It don't mean nothin'," or "It ain't no big thing." So our reaction to family situations, civilian crises, and life in general becomes either hypercontrol and order-and-harmony on one extreme, or "It don't mean nothin'" on the other. Our families live between these two extremes. Even when we're acting as rationally as we can (in our condition), our family suffers.

In Nam, we learned that to get close to anyone was to ask for trouble. We were emotionally vulnerable to pain when we developed close relationships, and the chances were great that that relationship would end suddenly in an ambush or booby trap. One moment I could be standing there talking to a friend, and the next I'm wearing his brains on the front of my shirt. In order to maintain any control of sanity, we had to freeze our senses. When we wanted to scream or strike out at someone or something for causing us to lose our closest friend, we couldn't. There was no answer except to make ourselves "hard core" to anything emotional or sensitive. It didn't even do any good to cry.

I've worked in many sales jobs and found it easier than most people. Some people consider me somewhat brilliant in sales. I found it easy because I could deal with people on a superficial level. I never had to build extended personal relationships because I always had someone else who would service customers on a long-term basis. Unlike most people, I always felt more comfortable around strangers than around my family and friends, because I never had to get into a deep relationship or justify myself for being weird on certain subjects. This put a strain on my family and is probably one reason I went from one sexual partner to another and am in my third marriage.

By working hard to suppress our emotions in order to "control ourselves," we have learned to display a deceptive meekness around others. This obvious attempt to correct our actions through an artificial softness and caring is a mask that covers a seething rage to strike out. Our families, who are close enough to see beneath the mask, are terrified of what they observe there.

The war experience has affected our lives, our children's lives, and the way families are being raised today. Four to five generations have already been affected by PTSD from Vietnam, but the family remains a weak second on the Veterans Administration's list of priorities. Our problem is one of time lag. We haven't been in combat for decades, yet we still react with survival tactics. Our families are paying a heavy price for a war long gone.

PTSD and the Midlife Crisis

A real eye-opener caught up with me a short time after I began working with Vietnam veterans. In my search for vets, I was unconsciously looking for guys in their twenties, strong and in good shape. The movie *Platoon* had just hit the local theaters, and it gave me a golden opportunity to seek fellow vets. I stood at the door of the movie house and watched for likely veterans as the crowds exited. I would approach them with a brochure I had written.

As the theater emptied out, I would zero in on someone with an army field-jacket or a camouflage shirt or hat. I quickly learned that these weren't the clues to look for. Instead, I had to check for the graying beard, the slight pouching around the waist, and the deep creased lines on the face caused by years of alcohol, drugs, or prevalent worry. When I realized I had been looking for the wrong age group, I had to laugh at myself. My brothers were middle-aged, and I hadn't noticed it until then! Though we still keep our teenage memories alive, we are not kids anymore.

What we're up against now is midlife change, compounded by the persistent effects of PTSD. I don't have a background in psychology or psychiatry, so I can't make any concrete pronouncements on the subject, but a few laymen's observations may help someone who is more qualified to take this on as a study.

During the period of a man's midlife change, certain desires become the central focus, controlling his thoughts and actions with a nearly overpowering influence. It is a time when masculinity appears at a turning point. The man looks in the mirror and wonders, "Am I still the man I used to be?" He may begin to wear teenage clothing styles, gold chains around his neck, unbuttoned shirts that allow his chest hairs to be fully seen, and more fashionable hairstyles. His attention goes to driving sports cars or something with flash, so that younger women will notice him. In short, he attempts to revert to years when he was a virile young man with no worries and with strength to take on the world. He also reverts to "toys" (motorcycles, boats, etc.) and actions that identify him as a young stud on the make.

If this reversion syndrome is a substantial trait of men in midlife crisis, how does it affect the Vietnam veteran?

Not long ago, I was in Canada and met a veteran by the name of Gavin. (There are nearly forty-five thousand Canadian vets who served in the US Armed Forces in Vietnam.) He was a clean-cut executive type with a tweed sports jacket and graying temples. He should have had a pipe in his mouth, but didn't. Gavin told me that recently he'd had the sudden urge to buy an M-14 rifle like the one he had used in Nam.

We had quite a laugh about his urge. But then he told me he had purchased the weapon and found great pleasure in shooting it. Was it PTSD or midlife crisis that caused Gavin, a most unlikely candidate, to develop this impulse to buy an M-14? I believe Gavin's experience was a midlife reversion to a time when he felt that the only security he had was in the possession of that weapon.

I've known many veterans who have bought army field-jackets, jungle fatigues, insignia, and all the assorted paraphernalia when they got into their middle age. And I've heard them say, "Well, what do you know, I'm finally getting some pride back, because now I want to wear my medals and uniform that I wouldn't wear when I got home." I believe the restoration of pride is part of it, but I think that the strong mental pictures of youthful virility play a large part in their buying habits.

At an age (seventeen, eighteen, nineteen years old) when the adult mind is still developing, we had our lives interrupted. Our adult personality developmental process came to a halt for nearly an entire year, and the only thing that mattered then was survival. This disruption caused many unresolved problems when we tried to resume normal life as young men. Now that most of us are in our fifties, we have another problem to face at a critical time of our lives: the inevitable change of life. If we don't find a way to put our teenage PTSD in remission while we're still in mid-life, we will probably carry its effects with us into old age.

THE STEPS TO RECOVERY

What can you do to help your family? Here are four suggestions:

1. Have them read this book. To my amazement, much of what's in this book comes as a total surprise to many people. Having your partner and older children read these chapters will inform them about your condition and relieve them from the uncertainty of not knowing why you are the way you are. It will open the door for the next step.

2. Talk through how your family can live with PTSD. Your family needs to become its own support unit. I cannot overemphasize this point. They need to be able to share feelings they may have never expressed to anyone—feelings about what their lives have been like as a result of living with a post-traumatically distressed husband or father. They have experienced specific fears, inhibitions, angers, and resentments in their home life. When their emotions resurface and they recapture memories of these things, it's important for them to hear that other family members have had the same or similar problems, and they too have never communicated these things because they feared the repercussions. If you allow (better yet, encourage) this to happen, all of a sudden your whole family will realize that they haven't been alone in the silent terror each of them has been experiencing. This opening up is the first step in removing the isolation that, for years, has stymied the free expression of love in your family. Among us, we have an unwritten rule to never speak about our war experiences. So don't try, at least at first. Instead, deal with the "hot spots"

in your family life. Work as a group to help each other. Here are a few specific ideas to help create a support unit in your family.

A) Everyone in your family should participate, because each one has a personal need. Your agenda is auto-biographical sharing. While you can't force your wife and kids to try it, their mutual need should be obvious. This commitment to work together around a common need will help bond you together.

B) Everyone should participate in the discussion freely, without criticism or judgment by others. Your feelings are genuine. So are those of your partner and children. They are feelings worthy of respect. Practice this principle as you talk through your trigger points, memories, and hurts.

C) Expect to be helped and to help. As you give of yourself, others receive. As they give, you receive. This is a life principle your family will pick up by osmosis. In so doing, they will find encouragement and release from their fears, frustrations, and guilt.

3. Your family support group should be facilitated by a trusting outsider. Think of someone who is a sensitive and skilled listener. This person should meet with you solely for the purpose of keeping the family on track in dealing with the issues at hand. Your group meeting is not a place to wage family squabbles of the ordinary sort. It is a place to reveal and release the repression, hidden hostilities, and pains that stem from your experiences in the war. Your facilitator should prod you into group discussions of what is and has been going on in your family life.

4. Along with organizing your family members into an effective support unit to deal with their familial

problems surrounding PTSD, it is good to introduce your family to another veteran family who is going or has gone through the same things. Not only does this get the family together with themselves (maybe for the first time ever in sincere conversation), but also it begins to allow them, as a unified group, to reach out of their isolated shell to others whom they can relate to, and vice versa.

This is the beginning of a very positive journey for your family. When they realize they aren't alone with their problems, and that what they have gone through is common in veteran families, they will begin to cast off their guilt, shame, and hostilities. Healing will be in store.

CHAPTER 10
_____

"Self-Medication"

★ ★ ★

I THINK THE WAR STARTED *creeping back into my life before I ever knew it. The lack of sleep really took its toll. I was fuzzy-headed every morning and exhausted by mid-afternoon. I just couldn't sleep because that same nightmare would get all over me every time I closed my eyes. One night, I opened one of the bottles of whiskey a friend had given us for Christmas. I wasn't a drinker, but after downing a pretty stiff "belt," I fell asleep. For the first time since coming back from Nam, I slept the night through without "gooks" in black pajamas crawling all over my face. I finally found relief, and soon was up to a fifth of whiskey a day.*

—A Vietnam vet with a sleep disorder

Vietnam was a war born in the psychedelic era. At a time when the Beatles graduated from "I Wanna Hold Your Hand" to "I am the Walrus" ("Everybody smoke pot, smoke pot, smoke pot"), and the "in" people sought peace, tranquility, and love through the inspiration of drugs, thousands of American teenagers were displaced into a primeval culture where anything went and very little was against the law. Drugs were everywhere. The Vietnamese built their houses out of marijuana plants. *Mamasan* sold it rolled and hermetically sealed in American cigarette packs. The black market thrived on sales of amphetamines, heroin, opium, and other highly addictive drugs to us young GIs, who needed to feel better or forget about the hell into which we had been dropped.

THE DRUG OF CHOICE

Although many American soldiers were subjected to numerous narcotic substances, and we ingested our share, we have chosen alcohol as the main drug we now use to medicate ourselves from the oppressive symptoms of PTSD. It is estimated that 30 percent of all Vietnam veterans still refuse to admit they were ever in Vietnam, and one of the ways we have submerged our experience is by self-medication with alcohol.

The numbing effect of alcohol has a tendency to ward off the flashbacks, depression, anxiety, and explosive fits of rage to which so many of us are prone. Many of us claim that alcohol is the one way we can get control of "something" that is uncontrollable in our lives. We can mask symptoms of PTSD with inebriation.

Alcohol is more accessible and cheaper than other drugs. We got used to relying on it early in our training. On military bases, the PX beer gardens provided a sanctuary for the homesick and nervous recruits. When, as teenagers, we joined the armed forces, we moved away from home, were harassed by harsh disciplines and harsher instructors, and were confined in an environment over which we had virtually no control. The one thing made available to us in our basic training—as a reward for passing inspections, good scores on tests, etc.—was a frequent trip to the PX beer halls and service clubs. There we discovered alcohol to be effective in reducing the stress we felt in our new and threatening surroundings.

Each of us received a weekly ration of beer while in Nam, compliments of Uncle Sam. When we returned from successful combat missions, each soldier was rewarded with an increase in his beer ration, just as we had been rewarded with trips to the PX if we scored high on the rifle range back at Fort Ord, California.

With the frustrations of a guerrilla war and a tendency to lose our tempers because of the futility of fighting an unseen enemy, we found alcohol to be an agent in diffusing the situation. Further, it made socializing under extremely suppressing social conditions bearable. Many of us found consuming alcohol a way to maintain rapport with other people, no matter what the conditions. Since the war, we have found that alcohol helps us suppress antisocial behavior (fighting, temper tantrums, etc.) and post-traumatic stress disorder.

Our Magical Formula for Coping

"You can't forget . . . but booze makes it go away for a while." This is a general consensus among Vietnam veterans who "drink for peace." The long, hard march through each night of terror can be made only with the numbing effect of alcohol.

Recently, while helping street people in Seattle, a friend of mine met four Vietnam veterans who had been living in the streets of various cities since returning from Nam. They related to him an interesting form of "bush" psychology, which they used in relation to drinking and getting drunk. It was a pure form of survivalism brought home from the war.

They had agreed long ago that only two of the four would drink at a time. One day two would get drunk, and the others would watch after them to keep them out of harm's way. The next day, they would switch. This is typical of the special brotherhood that developed over keeping each other alive in Nam. For these four vets, allowing their buddies the sanctity and safety of drinking to numb their nightmares was a form of warm sacrifice and compassion for their brothers. It was what they had practiced twenty years before in a land where they had been forgotten, and where they had learned that alcohol was the magical formula to help them cope.

Many of us have been using alcohol as a basic stress-reducing tool since the war and find it difficult to abandon now. Consequently, a large number of us have become alcoholics, and like all nonconfronting alcoholics, we are extremely resistant to seek out treatment in order to give it up. Rather than find the way to health, we rely upon self-medication to deal with our symptoms. Ultimately, we'll pay the price, we know. Even sadder is the fact that those we love will also have to share in that cost . . . even as they are sharing in it now.

THE PILL PROBLEM

I recently talked with a vet who claimed that, after spending one year in treatment at a local VA hospital, he was hooked on pills they had doled out to help him cope with his PTSD. He named four antidepressants: Nardil for his depression, Doxepin and Trazodone for his sleep disturbance, and Lorazepam for his anxiety.

He told me that he kept all of the plastic bottles the pills had come in, and after a year had nearly filled up two plastic garbage bags with these containers. He said that he and a friend were in the process of using these empties to make a shrine in his home. He was sure they had enough between them to make four solid walls to cover an entire room in his house. The sad part was that he still suffered from major symptoms of PTSD and was very bitter about his treatment at the hands of the government.

As with any kind of sedating effect, using massive doses of antidepressants can develop unpleasant side effects and a leaning toward dependency. Vietnam veterans who repeatedly go to a chemical buffer and see no light at the end of the tunnel, determine that it is better to be a slave to a drug that knocks them out than to live with the mental horrors stuffed away in their heads.

Alcohol and pills tend to exaggerate one's personality in opposite directions. Alcohol usually acts as a trigger to overtly respond in a physically violent manner to a stressful situation. In our society, it is acceptable to exhibit personality changes when intoxicated with alcohol. Whether or not we're veterans, people appear to regard it as socially OK to move from timidity to bravado when we're drunk. Pills such as barbiturates, tranquilizers, and opiates tend to cause us to space out so much that our personality changes to one of deep withdrawal (unless we overdose on barbiturates).

A veteran under the influence of alcohol can expect to be more overt in his communication, more aggressive in discharging his built-up stress, and he may even force his stress upon those around him as a style of controlled relief. A vet being manipulated by the effects of pills will usually find a false peace of mind and retreat from social confrontations. He may even begin to deny that his problems are war-related. We have a "strong," bullying reaction to alcohol. Pills cause a "weak" response of insecurity and self-denunciation. In either case, self-medicating brings temporary relief, at best.

THE FAMILY SUFFERS

Not surprisingly, wife battering and child abuse are characteristic among veterans who use alcohol and other drugs to medicate themselves out of the inner war. Our children often suffer from PTSD symptoms similar to our own. They live in fear that they may set us off. They become depressed, and many develop behavioral problems with their peers.

In the last chapter, I stated that we can be overprotecting and overdemanding, while at the same time finding it difficult to be close with our children. Many of us find that the only time we can be "real" with our families is when we mellow ourselves with drugs and alcohol. I can remember how I used to have some of my greatest moments of closeness and affinity with my children after smoking marijuana. The problems of life and the children's idiosyncrasies would fall away, and I would relax with them. The only thing was that they weren't stoned, so it was tough for them to believe I was sincere in my feelings.

If you are stoned, you can still emote (react with fabricated or dramatic emotions), but these feelings are not real. Life becomes something that lives on the "other side" of the place where you live. You are bodily in a place, but through drinking and drugging you are emotionally distant, and the people you have to deal with will hopefully never know the difference. Many of us have become experts at this false show of emotion, but it is a short-lived relief. The stuff of real life, real feelings and relationships, quickly catches up with us.

Often our wives become protective of us and take over the chore of parenting. They begin to "mother" us, and if drinking or drugging makes us mellow out, then they sometimes become an ally, encouraging us to self-medicate even more. Eventually, they will believe that there is no problem at all. They accept and overlook our drinking and drugging. This may go on for a time, before our inability to recover from our social problems gets so out of hand that our entire family is forced to face the situation, or before outside intervention becomes necessary. While it may appear that self-medication is not such a bad compromise—that it is a reasonable way to alleviate our pain—in the end, it compounds the difficulty of our mental, physical, and emotional recovery.

UNABLE TO CONTROL OUR HABITS

It is common for many of us to attempt to control our alcohol problem by cutting down on consumption. Often, however, we end up drinking more to handle the combined stress of keeping sober and of suppressing the war problems, which quickly reemerge. By self-medicating—trying to handle our depression, intrusive thoughts, and hypervigilance alone, with no outside help—we get caught up in a roller-coaster ride of increasing and decreasing our consumption to the point of no return. It seems that each time we decrease our drinking or we go "on the wagon," we have to use a larger amount of alcohol to regain control of our life once we decide to begin consumption again. We cannot summon enough willpower to control alcohol the way we desire. This roller-coaster ride, as we try to overcome our past problems, results in our dependency upon alcohol. We become alcoholics.

A very popular method of self-medication is to switch from alcohol to other drugs, such as marijuana and downers. These drugs seem to unleash even more PTSD symptoms because the numbing effect of alcohol departs, and we again become sensitized to our environment. The end result is that we drink more alcohol to get numb again.

A nonconfronting alcoholic cannot face his addiction and therefore denies he has a problem. Many of us do that. This complicates our denial of having been damaged by the war, or even having been there at all. The denial symptoms of alcoholism and PTSD work together until we are living in an unreal world, a mental no-man's-land. Our feelings of worthlessness, guilt, and social rejection already have us believing we are outsiders. Admitting we are controlled by alcohol or another drug, puts us deeper in the foxhole.

Alcoholics Anonymous maintains that until alcoholics hit rock-bottom, admitting their lives are out of control, there is little hope of any change. Admitting that we have a problem is an all-important first step in the right direction.

STEPS TO RECOVERY

Here are four steps you can take to move toward a life free of the need for self-medication:

1. Again, admit that you have a problem. You can't get help until you admit that you need it. If you habitually drink or take drugs in order to suppress thoughts and feelings about Nam, you are chemically dependent. If you continually need drugs or alcohol to get through work or social interaction, it is obvious that these things are controlling you, rather than you controlling them. Your self-medication is itself proof that you are wounded. Admit it, friend. Ad-

mit it to yourself and your family. You will not be able to defeat your PTSD symptoms until you get rid of your dependency upon alcohol and drugs. Do yourself a favor for a change. Acknowledge you are out of control.

2. Get professional help. Once you admit you have a problem, it is time to get help by submitting to detoxification and/or medical treatment. There are dozens of agencies that deal with this, including many hospitals. They will give you medical attention and counseling for you and your family. It's a tough step to take, but a necessary one. You can do it. You did much harder things during the war!

3. Make some solid agreements that you'll quit for good. Make these agreements first with yourself and then with others who care about you. There is no room for leniency here. You are declaring war against yourself, and your agreements had better be firm if you intend to come out the victor (and you do intend to win!) Ask your loved ones to cooperate in helping you recognize your lies—all alcoholics and addicts are liars—so you can face these lies head-on.

It is important to place yourself in a support system, such as a support group. Once you have given up alcohol or drugs, you have to replace them with a good program that addresses PTSD and problems you have acquired from the Vietnam War. Point Man, the organization I work with, is one of your best options, because it is made up of other Nam vets who have gone through the same things. We know where you're coming from, and we know where you've been. We also know what really works to bring lasting relief.

4. Recognize that you are responsible for the condition you are in. While you cannot change what happened to you in Vietnam, you are responsible for who you are *now*. The fact is, you survived, and you were brought home from the war for a reason. You survived a year of horrors and lived for the dream of coming home. Now you are here. Wounded maybe, but here. You can make your life good again. It is true. I've seen it happen to myself and to many other veterans I know. I believe that deep, deep inside, you yearn for a healthy, normal life again. So put away the pill bottles and liquor. There is a way out of PTSD that is neither destructive nor self-suppressive. It is the way to find who you really were meant to be.

And that leads me to tell you more about myself. My life has run the gamut—everything from hiding in the woods, taking drugs, and a near-massacre of innocent people, being trained by the CIA, blowing away two marriages, and my present work to help other Nam vets. I'm not proud of much of my life since I came back from Vietnam, but it's better now. Much better. I've found peace and love again, and I'm doing something I find deeply rewarding.

CHAPTER 11

My Story

★ ★ ★

THE EVENING HAZE WAS misty green as shadows grew longer along the chaparral lacing the hill. We walked along, overlooking the long valley, discussing what had happened.

"I say we dust them all off!"

Fontana jammed a seven-round magazine into his .308. "I ain't going to let no jive-ass hippie tell me what I can eat and what I can't."

I looked at his face and turned my gaze away quickly. The LSD we had taken several hours earlier was definitely supreme stuff. The four of us had been up and "off" now for hours, without any indication that the drug was wearing off.

Popcorn sat down with a crumpled sound and propped his rifle against a dry, bleached, rotting log. He began rolling a cigarette from his makin's. Kurt began to gather firewood, and without any verbal announcement, the four of us began preparing a camp on top of the gentle slope.

The Chilcotin of central British Columbia was a long way from the jungles and paddies of Southeast Asia, but we instinctively took precautions to ensure that our position was in no way compromised by a hostile force. The LSD heightened our preparedness, which most people would have called paranoia.

A thin trail of smoke climbed into the pale, green evening from the small, log farmhouse in the valley below. Mist was already forming in the large pasture behind the rustic structure, and I could hear the faint barking from one of the dogs. Papa John and friends had used the place for almost four years. They paid no rent but managed to trade enough drugs to the landowner to use the farm as a commune.

Papa John had a good heart. He allowed almost anything to go down on the farm. He never got riled up because the four of us kept weapons. He never got tiffed if one of us decided to shack up with one of his girlfriends or his wife. He was a man of peace and free love, so why not? He never was overly upset to find out that I had been hunting grouse and rabbits to eat, as long as we ate them away from the commune and didn't make a big issue out of it.

The straw that broke his easygoing nature was the day I brought a dead bird into the kitchen, blood still dripping from its headless neck, when the "friends" were "omming" a prayer over their evening mush. I had been out of my right mind from three joints of marijuana and a six-pack of Labatt's.

I swung the limp grouse over my head in a wide, arching circle, spewing fresh blood over everyone in the room, yee-hawing in rebel style. I was fed up with their vegetarian diet and decided to let them all know. The next day, Papa John asked me to leave.

As darkness fell on the slope, we settled down to get into each other's heads. The firelight jostled shadows around Fontana's face.

"That Papa-dude's got to go, man," he said. "I say we fire up that whole farm, just like we did in Nam." Fontana was making sense—or I should say, the LSD was. We found ourselves unanimously agreeing that we should take the hippies out.

We had left the farm in the morning, after Papa John had asked me to hit the road. The other three men had come with me because we were "brothers." We were tight and looked after each other, finding comfort in being with other guys who understood our way of life. The four of us had been getting stoned together for about six months, and had come to trust each other as much as Nam vets could trust anyone. We didn't look much different from ordinary hippies—we all had shoulder-length hair and wore denim jeans and jackets. But one thing was different. We never went anywhere individually or as a group unless we were armed.

When we had come back from Nam, we couldn't wait for our hair and beards to grow long, so we could blend into society without being singled out as GIs. We had felt vulnerable with short hair and clean-shaven cheeks in a world where our peers identified each other with how long they could grow their hair and beards. We had left the jungles and hostile rice paddies, where we had learned to camouflage ourselves for self-preservation. So we learned to adapt to our surroundings, and life in America in the '60s was only a different jungle. But even though we looked like hippies, you could have sensed that we were on edge. Danger was before and around us.

Kurt poked into the fire with a stick. "I don't think we'll get any resistance," he said, "so SOP tactics won't be needed.

All we've gotta do is walk in there, take them out, and fire the place up. Simple."

He gazed into the fire and went on. "I mean it ain't like Nam, man. These are just a bunch of peace freaks that don't even know that it's possible to die. Hell, we'd never have a fire out in plain sight like this in Nam."

We talked and smoked through the night. Popcorn unloaded and reloaded his weapon at least six times through the eerie, acid-laced darkness. Once he got onto a trip of shining the bullets on his pant leg. When he was through, they glistened in the firelight.

We conjured up at least two or three reasons, for the good of humanity, to kill each person who was staying in the farmhouse. Their lives could not go on the way they lived. And besides, someone, somewhere, would take them out because they were so weak and vulnerable. We were not only doing the world a favor by weeding out the weak, as a wolf pack does to the caribou herds up north, we were doing the hippies a favor as well.

Before sunrise, we rolled out, kicked the fire into a pile of smoldering coals, and started down the slope toward the farm. Our weapons were ready, as was our resolve. Suddenly, a green Travelall truck pulled up on the road in front of the farm, and we halted our descent.

"Hey, it's your old lady, Chuck!" Fontana said. "I thought she was in Vancouver."

With the sight of the green truck, something happened to me. I instantly realized that I didn't want to kill anybody. I just wanted to be in that truck with Sally, riding off somewhere away from there.

She had left me two weeks earlier because I had wanted to shack up with another chick at the farm. Sally was three months pregnant, and I thought to have a safe pregnancy it was best for her to get down to Vancouver and out of these hills before the snow fell. So in my usual fashion of running someone off without losing my cool, I simply began to live with another woman in the big house. Sally got angry and left. Mission accomplished. Now here she was, and I suddenly realized that she was my safe harbor, and I didn't want any part of commune life and the people involved. They accepted, and we filed down the hill and greeted my pregnant wife, who gladly took me back as she had so many countless times before.

Disaster averted. That was in June, 1969, two years after I walked away from the US Army.

First Combat Unit in Action

In February of 1963, about the time the Beatles were making their first appearance on the Ed Sullivan show, I stood staring at a life-size poster cutout in the window of the army recruiting office in Centralia, Washington. I was awestruck by the figure in the poster. He was tall, clean shaven. The most rugged looking man I'd ever seen in a military uniform.

His dark green "class A" uniform was perfect. The peaked garrison cap cocked on his head bore the round parachute and glider patch, but it was his boots which led me into the tiny recruiting station and kept me there for the next two hours. They were spit-shined beyond belief, and the dress uniform's pant legs were tucked inside of them. Did that look sharp, or what? No other branch of the service had the privilege of wearing jump boots with their dress uniform, and that sold me on becoming a paratrooper. I had always wanted to be original, to maybe do something my older brother wouldn't do, since I seemed to be expected to follow in his footsteps. I could go into the Marine Corps, but they didn't do anything much different than the regular army. Jumping out of planes would definitely set me apart.

So, after enlisting for a three-year tour, I was sent to Fort Ord. Then I was shipped off to Fort Benning, Georgia, for six weeks of jump school. There, we learned how to exit from the military's worst-maintained aircraft, at two thousand feet, but the actual jumping was only a week long. The prior five weeks were grueling hours of living hell. Boot camp was like a summer vacation compared to jump school. My class began with over eleven hundred men from every branch of the armed forces. It ended with around six hundred. Since airborne is strictly voluntary, we could quit any time during the training and be reassigned. The object of our instructors was to make us quit in the first few weeks. I wanted to, every hour during the six weeks.

Upon graduation from jump school, I was assigned to the 82d Airborne Division at Fort Bragg, North Carolina. I was restless. The Cuba invasion at the Bay of Pigs was long gone, and I wanted to see some action. I was gung ho to win some medals, but there was no war. Life lingered on with pulling guard duty and KP, with senseless inspections and drunken nights in Fayetteville.

One day I met a new man who had arrived from duty in Okinawa. He had a red-and-yellow patch on his right shoulder, and sported a combat infantry badge over his jump wings. He said that while serving with the 173d Airborne Brigade on Okinawa, he was sent over to a place called Vietnam to be a door gunner on a helicopter for thirty days. He described life on Okinawa as having no guard duty, no KP, and a chance to get involved in a war and get some combat decorations without the long-term commitment to the drudgery of a war. It looked good to me, so I found myself in front of the career counselor the next day, reenlisting for an extra year so I could go to Okinawa with the 173d Airborne Brigade.

We spent the next year jungle training on Okinawa, Taiwan, the Philippines, and various other rain islands in the South China Sea. Life was good. Our unit was tight, and we got to know each other very well. We were prepared and stayed on a readiness status as a reactionary force for the entire Asian theater.

In May of 1965, President Johnson ordered us onto C-1 aircraft. We were deployed into South Vietnam as the first regular combat unit to enter the war. We were told we would be in South Vietnam for a temporary duty assignment of sixty days. We were to sweep into areas where no free forces had ever gone, secure them, turn them over to the control of the South Vietnamese Army, and return to Okinawa.

We were excited. Here was our chance to do a little fighting, win a few medals, and then get back safe and sound.

But it didn't work that way.

After our temporary duty, we were extended indefinitely to South Vietnam. Other army divisions and units began to arrive, and we knew the good life was over. The little bit of jungle rot, malaria, and rotten conditions were going to be with us for a long time to come. Our "temporary" assignment was the first of many lies to come from our government.

The Lucky Ones Died

It was two o'clock in the morning, and the temperature was still hovering around the 90s. We had turned in our weapons and gear the previous day, and were confined to this tiny, barbed-wire compound on Tan Son Nhut Airbase for a day and a half. After thirty cans of beer each, the thirty or so troopers crowded into the little space and scrounged for a place to sleep.

Our plane, a commercial jet airliner, would be arriving and leaving in four hours. We were going back to the world. Our war was over, and now everything would be made right again. It felt as if we were on the upward yank of someone dunking us in a toilet for twelve months. Home was only a few hours away. Unbelievable.

I'd managed to find a mattress inside the semblance of a building, corrugated tin and scrap wood thrown together. I was on the brink of slipping into a drunken stupor when the frightening concussion of mortar explosions knocked me to the ground. I instinctively threw the mattress over me as explosions ripped through the tiny compound. At first, I pounded my fists into the ground in anger and yelled, "You're not going to get me, Charlie! I'm too short! You're not gonna get me now, Charlie!"

And then I broke. I sobbed out to God: "Oh, God, I've been through too much to get taken out now. Just let me go home. Please."

As suddenly as it had begun, the explosions ceased. My thoughts of God vanished in the confusion, heightened by the drunken condition of everyone in the compound. I heard the wounded crying out and someone vainly screaming to his dead friend to get up. I threw off the shrapnel-riddled mattress and went to a wounded GI nearby. His stomach was gashed open. I ripped off my T-shirt and applied it to the wound, yelling for a medic.

Seven teenage soldiers died that morning in the tiny compound halfway around the world. After spending a year in hell, this was their reward. How unjust it seemed! But after coming home and seeing how we were received by the people who had sent us to fight, I thought that they were the lucky ones. They escaped the war after Vietnam. We did not.

AMONG THE ALIENS

Eighteen hours from that dirty little compound of death, terror, and heartache, I found myself in a mystical, dream-like place called San Francisco Airport.

As I walked through the crowd, I was amazed. There were so many clean people. The mingled fragrances of perfume and cologne were nearly overwhelming to a nose that for two years had only smelled decaying fish, human waste, gunpowder, and pungent Asian food.

As I stumbled through the masses of clean people, I caught bits and pieces of conversation:

"Oh, I dunno. I'll take a Jag over a Mercedes any day . . ."

"I like the large refrigerator. You know—the one with the double doors and ice-maker . . ."

"Just got back from Big Bear. Skiing's great up there right now . . ."

It was a strange, alien language. These people, whom I had spent two years dreaming of rejoining, were now foreigners to me. Though my adrenaline was still running on fast-motion from my recent brush with death, these people didn't seem to be aware that there was a war going on, right that moment. And if they did know about the war, none of them cared about my brothers who were dying that instant in some dark, stinking jungle on the other side of the world.

I began to lose my bearings. A deep confusion settled in. Finding a lonely corner near my assigned gate, I squatted with my back to the wall and mentally walked through my course of action should any of these "foreigners" invade my space. I was alone again but would survive at all costs. All my childhood dreams of being a war hero, with a grateful country cheering me on, blew up in my mind. I was not only ignored, but sensed I had become an outcast from the very people who had sent me to do what they had asked me to do—for them.

After spending the next few months of my remaining enlistment in Seattle with a military police detachment, I was honorably discharged from the US Army. I had spent four of the most critical years of my life surviving the military. Now I found myself confronted with the difficulties of adjusting to civilian life. I soon discovered that the only time I could put up with other people was when I was dead drunk. When that didn't work, I isolated myself and smoked pot until I became unconscious.

None of my friends were into pot, so when things got too stressed out, I would crawl off into my world of Deep Purple, the Rolling Stones, and the Beatles. Marijuana took my worries away, and my dark little apartment became an ideal sanctuary. I could control my environment when I was alone, but being around civilians, who didn't know how to be prepared for danger, drove me up the wall.

Three short months later, I entered another army recruiting station to reup for another hitch. I couldn't relate to anyone at home. I thought that maybe I could gradually find some peace with living in America again by using the army as a means to help me readjust. I could live off the military posts as a part-time civilian, and the stateside army would provide a safe harbor for me to run to when I couldn't tolerate the real world any longer.

I was assigned to Fort Ord, California, and my work was to continue as an MP, since that had been my last duty prior to discharge. At the replacement depot, they told me I would be guarding prisoners in the stockade. The last thing I needed was to follow a bunch of American prisoners around with a shotgun while they cleaned up trash around the post. "Besides," I told the first sergeant, "I don't trust myself with loaded weapons. I'll blow one of those guys away if he looks cross-eyed at me." They decided that my being a guard might not be a good idea after all, and gave me another choice.

The other choice came with a guarantee. If I took the duty assignment, I would not have to go back to Vietnam. That sounded pretty good since I hadn't reenlisted to spend another twelve months of burning leeches off my butt, constant diarrhea, and the threat of losing life or limb in a war that wasn't a war. That duty assignment meant becoming a drill instructor for basic training troops. I took it.

STONED, COURTESY OF UNCLE SAM

My next two years were a maze of conflicts, doubts, and further alienation. Every trainee became a little green machine, a number that looked exactly like the one standing beside it, or in rank behind it.

I avoided any personal relationships with these young men whom I was training for Vietnam, and I honestly believe my time as a drill instructor solidified many of my PTSD symptoms. Old fears arose—fears of getting too close to someone and then having him get killed or wounded. Consequently, I didn't want to know anything about the hundreds of teenagers whom I was sending to a distant land of terror, drugs, and pain, a land that would change their lives forever.

After my promotion to staff sergeant (E-6), I was given a buck sergeant as my assistant. This was the turning point in my relationship with the army, PTSD, and America. I moved off the post and into a small bungalow in Monterey. My assistant would get the troops up at five o'clock, take them on their morning run, have them clean the barracks, run them through the breakfast chow line, and get them ready for the day's training agenda. I would arrive around nine o'clock and take over from there, which consisted of marching them to their training stations, and then turning them over to my assistant while I drank coffee. (A number of years ago I attended the opening ceremonies in Sacramento, California, of the California Vietnam Veterans Memorial. While looking at all the names on those walls, I realized that well over one hundred of the names were soldiers I had personally trained. It was another step toward healing.)

During this time, I was spending most of my hours off-post with some hippie friends in Monterey's Cannery Row area. We talked philosophy, smoked pot, and shared "free love." My hair grew a little longer each day, and my mustache was completely against army regulations. I was soon known all over Fort Ord as "Sergeant Sunshine." It was not uncommon for me to march a squad of trainees out into the woods after dark, sit them down and share a "lid" of grass with them, telling them I was getting their heads ready for Nam. I did this without any emotion or desire to create personal relationships with them, because when I looked at them, I saw dead men.

After about a year and a half of this duty, I met a young woman who had hitchhiked up from Newport Beach. She spent the night with me and never left. We were married a month or so later.

It was at this point that I was introduced to LSD, and my bride and I were stoned on acid every weekend from that point forward. My head really took a turn from the military. One very unusual effect of LSD is that it seemingly turns one into an abstract thinker. War, the army, Vietnam, and society in general became targets for my ridicule and rejection. I retreated from them mentally and physically.

Something happened to my mind under the influence of that very potent drug, and it became obvious to my superiors at the post. Four months after my marriage (it was my second; I had been married previously as a high-school student), I received orders to Fort Bragg, North Carolina. I was assigned to the John F. Kennedy Special Forces Center, where I would undergo a course in Vietnamese language and unspecified "other" training. This could mean only one thing. I was on my way back to Nam. So much for my guarantee.

It was apparent that my superiors agreed I was out of control as a drill instructor. They obviously knew of my "liberal" attitudes and were probably aware of my hippie friends and drug abuse. So it was off to where they thought I belonged—on a special assignment in Vietnam, probably one from which I would never return.

My second day at Fort Bragg brought me to a decision I was to live with for many years to come. There were thirty or so high-ranking, noncommissioned officers in the course, most of whom had been to Nam before and now were either alcoholics, druggies like me, or violently out of control. As I looked around, I could see that the army had found a use for some of the damaged survivors of the Vietnam War: special assignments.

We were ushered into a large, barnlike building, and the door was locked with an MP posted outside. Inside, a civilian with a crewcut walked onto the stage and drew down a large map of North Vietnam. My heart leaped and sank at the same moment. We were not only going back to Vietnam, we were going back as CIA operatives to do some very ugly things to the Vietnamese and Americans.

I made the decision right then. I would not go. With my new hippie wife, I would leave the army and America before I would go back and murder people for the CIA.

CHAPTER 12

How I Made Peace with My Past

★ ★ ★

DESERTING.

Never, during six years in the Army, could I imagine myself going AWOL, let alone committing the ultimate military sin. My wife and I hooked up with many underground antiwar groups and used an "underground railroad" to get us across the Canadian border. There, we landed as immigrants, awaiting citizenship in a foreign country.

Our drug usage increased and our lifestyle deteriorated in the city of Vancouver, so with what little money we had saved, we hit the road, moving from one hippie commune to the next. Our lives were shattered, unreal. The drugs and free-love lifestyle we indulged in left us no hope that anything would get any better. Our beautiful world of sexual anything-goes, laced with psychedelic drugs, brought on some of my life's deepest depressions. The crash of coming down from a high made reality even more unbearable. With so little to dream about or hope for, we were committing a slow form of suicide.

After more than six years of adventures and misadventures, twelve marriage separations, and more than a few near-disastrous episodes like the one I described in the previous chapter, I went to Vancouver Airport and turned myself over to US Immigration authorities.

LIFE SIMPLY WASN'T WORKING

I was sent to Fort Benjamin Harrison, Indiana, where I was mustered out of the Army with an undesirable discharge. President Ford offered me amnesty if I would participate in the alternate service program. I chose to do so, and after completing my work assignment, my discharge was upgraded to a general discharge under honorable conditions. It all seemed a long way from War Zone D or the Iron Triangle, where so many of my young paratrooper friends went down and never got up.

LIKE TAKING OFF A ONE-HUNDRED-POUND RUCKSACK

As a result of my discharge status, guilt set in. I was no longer a military person, though I still thought like one. I didn't have any idea what kind of person I really was. I was a treacherous, unfeeling husband and as a result, my wife of thirteen years, finally accepted a divorce from me. My PTSD reaction of not allowing people to be close or to care about me was obviously out of control. I erased my second wife from my life with a good Mexican lawyer and a hundred-dollar bill. And left her also suffering from PTSD from just being married to me.

I vowed to myself that I would never get involved with a woman again. I didn't need the misery. So I threw myself into writing screenplays for a Hollywood production company. The only time I left my one-room, cockroach-infested apartment was to get some beer and cheap two-day-old chicken at the greasy little store next door.

Here I found a measure of release. I became obsessed with writing, and how I wrote. I discovered I could write down things I had wanted to say for years, and in doing so, I was actually finding release from past sufferings. Nobody ever wanted to read the stuff I wrote, let alone buy it. But I absolutely found joy in being alone and writing.

I titled the first complete work *Letters from Nam*, and the language was inclined to peel the paint off the walls. But I felt good when it was finally all out on paper. I was debriefing myself from thirteen years of bad cargo. I was starving half to death, but finding relief.

I continued to write, and more pus from Vietnam oozed out. By this time, I had become more interested in writing to debrief myself than to sell any of my screenplays or novelettes. I was sure that any publisher would have thrown them out anyway, so that's what I did—threw them all away. I would spend three days writing nonstop, just to throw it all away with a big sigh of relief. It felt as if I were taking off a hundred-pound rucksack a little at a time.

Uncharted Waters

About this time a miracle happened to me. A friend introduced me to a friend of hers. What a different person she was—strong, self-reliant, and beautiful. She was a successful business owner with so much class that she scared me half to death.

We began to see each other, and I believe the only thing that brought me out of my cockroach apartment was the intrigue I had for this interesting creature. She was definitely from an area of society I had never charted, but since she showed interest in me, I was going to ride it out, no matter what.

I would go shopping with her in her new BMW. I had never seen a woman shop for clothes with a shopping cart. She ripped and tore through long racks of the finest dresses at Bonwit Teller in Beverly Hills. Piles of dresses, and with a flick of her credit card she would walk out with what seemed like half the store. I followed and escorted her with my mouth gaping in amazement. It was a world I had never known, but I didn't plan to leave until she asked me to; it was too much fun to watch.

A month after meeting her, we fell in love. I had left my camera at her house the night before and returned to pick it up. When she came to the door, we both looked at each other and knew at that instant that for the rest of our lives we would never love anyone else the way we loved each other.

Athena became Mrs. Charles Dean on Valentine's Day, barely two months after we'd met. And another miracle happened: my wandering eyes and lust for other women ended as abruptly as a sudden-death ball game.

The Curse Returns

As we settled into marriage (my third), things had all the indications of being the best ever in my life. For the first three or four months, my war-related stress seemed to vanish, as a result of this new partnership with the woman of my dreams. But in time, the curse again reared its ugly head.

Athena had been raised in a home where no known relatives had gone to Vietnam. She had been a preteen, preoccupied with the comforts of a wealthy family. She had paid little attention to the place called Vietnam or what had happened there. In fact, it meant almost nothing to her when she found out a couple of months later that I was a Vietnam veteran. But when she began to see the stress re-emerging in my life, she became interested. She recognized that the man she had married had been deeply hurt, and his pain was beginning to affect the marriage.

Every time we went to a party where there was drinking and doping, I would overdo it. I drank and partied with a crazy flair she couldn't relate to. Anything-goes attitudes became more predominant in our social life, but she wasn't in agreement. My wild, drunken streaks of loud, boisterous fun were not fun to her.

In drunken states, I tried to communicate some stress-related thoughts to her. She gave me a blank stare and was disinterested. I would get drunk because it would give me a chance to be crazy and have an excuse for it. I can remember sitting on the floor beside our bed, drinking a full gallon of wine and muttering to myself after she had fallen asleep during one of my stress-related conversations. I actually found myself hating her for not having the interest to listen to me all night long.

Many times I would drink myself into a staggering mess. Then at four o'clock in the morning, I'd climb into my car and drive with blinding rage through the streets of Burbank or Los Angeles. I flew at dangerously excessive speeds down streets with cross streets. It's amazing that I didn't get arrested or killed. In reflection, I believe that I was trying hard either to kill myself or to provoke a cop to do it for me, because I know that if an officer had stopped me, I would have opposed him to the point of "it's either him or me."

These times of stress boil-over were instigated by my wife's disinterest in my problems. I would flare up and do obnoxious things just to make her notice, such as throw a jealous fit over her relationships years before we met. Out of self-pity, I created problems that were so crazy that she had to get interested. My insanity was surfacing, and I found myself in panicked states, trying to cover it up. The last person I wanted to have know about it was her.

The business that Athena and I worked to create became very successful. We both loved it in the beginning, but I soon became bored and began to step back from it. While we worked as a business team, we had much in common. Our married life bloomed. I had temper flare-ups occasionally, tripping out into times of needing isolation, but on the whole we were very happy.

Our marriage took on a different tone when I began showing disinterest in the business and stepping back and doing other things that weren't related to it, including more writing and painting. But it wasn't until we received a promotion and moved to Seattle that things became really bad.

A NEW FANATICISM

In Seattle, I went off the deep end when I got together with an old friend, a Vietnam veteran. We were involved in an organization that protested taxes and that radically opposed the current government structure. This "patriot" movement really hit a chord with me, and I soon became a fanatic.

Athena, a conservative person who rarely likes to rock the boat, soon found herself married to a man on the verge of going to jail. I felt I needed to change the government, the tax system, license system, and every other system connected with modern American life. In a period of three months, I submitted affidavits to all branches of the government, revoking my driver's license, social-security number, marriage license, and fishing license. I sent them all back and declared myself a natural-born citizen of the United States, who did not need to be licensed to be a citizen. I returned my license plate to the secretary of state and mounted my own that said, "Just Skip It." When I would get stopped by the police I would tell them that I wasn't required to have a license plate or driver's license because I was a natural individual and citizen of the United States. I never got a ticket or trip to jail. The officers were either confused or didn't want to bother with me.

During the course of a year, Athena threatened several times to kick me out. When the IRS and state's attorney came to visit, that snapped the camel's back. I had been running a fundraising business through a "warehouse" bank, which kept few records. When it got raided, everyone with an account got a visit. Athena told me that it was all over, and she wanted a divorce. This devastated me. I knew she was the best thing I had ever had in my life. She had caused so many positive changes in me, and here I was committing another relational suicide with the best woman in the world.

After about a week of freaking out, stressing out, insomnia, and really going crazy inside, I broke down and called a friend in Burbank. Bill was in the same business as Athena and had helped us many times before. So for some reason, I felt he was the only one who could possibly help restore our broken relationship. I called him and simply said, "Bill, I really need a friend right now."

He was quiet for a moment and then replied, "Chuck, you need the Lord."

His statement stunned me. A week earlier, I might have laughed, but at that moment, with my life in shambles, something inside told me that what he was saying was true, that here was the answer I'd been seeking, though outwardly avoiding for years. I straightened up in the chair, wiped my nose, and brushed the tears from my red, swollen eyes. "Yeah," I said softly. "I guess that's one thing I haven't tried. Maybe that's what I need to do."

Bill talked with me for a little while, then asked if I was willing to pray with him. I agreed, because I knew that the way I was headed could only end in disaster. Then and there, over long distance "Ma Bell," I prayed with him, giving my heart, soul, and life to the Lord Jesus Christ.

When I got off the phone, I didn't hear angels singing or rockets going off. But I felt different. I didn't have any glitzy TV or Hollywood-hyped religious experience. But there was a peace in my mind I hadn't felt before, a sense of release far beyond any of my writer's dumps. Gradually, I realized that I had been inducted into a new army—heaven's.

I also knew that I had been the cause of the marriage problems between Athena and me, and I was willing to move out of her life if that would give her more peace. I didn't expect or demand anything from anyone anymore, because in an instant God had filled my inner void, the secret desire that I had never known existed until I surrendered all my problems to Him. I was now what I had always told myself I would never be: a Christian. But I now understood that a Christian is a person remade by God into a new, eternal, joyous being. I knew that whatever happened now, it would be all right. I would be all right. This calming, secure sensibility replaced the feelings of death, fear, and agony that I had experienced and expected to experience for the rest of my life.

Lives Get Fixed

Although we were working out the details of separation and divorce, Athena and I still lived together during this time. We had agreed that I could live there while preparing to move back to California. After my phone conversation with Bill and the resulting change in my life, I spoke with her briefly and told her I was no longer resisting the split-up. I said she would always be my favorite person in the world, and all that I wanted for her was a peaceful and prosperous life.

Perplexed by the gentleness that had suddenly come over me, she discovered that I had talked with Bill. After I left, she called him to find out what was going on. Athena had never had much exposure to God, Jesus Christ, or the church. Her father was a professing atheist, and she grew up with virtually no religious background. So when Bill told her I had asked Jesus to come into my life and save me, she laughed.

"Chuck a Christian? You've gotta be joking! That's the last thing I'd ever expect from him."

I prayed that God would fix the mess I'd made of our marriage. Two days later, He put His big hand in the middle of our lives and smoothed out all the ugly wrinkles. We were on a trip back from a business retreat, and Athena was inflexible about the divorce. As we talked, she found out that her secretary (and her secretary's boyfriend) were planning on joining me in a new business venture in California. She realized that her secretary had instigated many of our fights and began to see where our problems were coming from. Her heart softened, and we were restored as husband and wife. All the divorce plans whisked away forever. Three weeks later, Athena asked the Lord to forgive her and enter her life. Seeing her transformed as I had been added to the miracle that had happened in my life.

Our restored marriage was the beginning of the healing God had in store for me. I soon found out that He had erased my long dread of dying; I had been in four years of trauma about the idea of my death. My urge to drink and use dope vanished abruptly. The heavy symptoms of my PTSD felt like part of another life that I had once lived but now was dead and gone. The nightmares and horrible mental pictures of the war had been transferred from my present self to the former Chuck, the dead person who was no longer part of my new life. It was as if Jesus had taken all the mental images from my subconscious mind and mounted them in a photo album. I could still see them from time to time, but they no longer impinged on my life or dictated the symptoms of post-traumatic stress disorder. I had finally found peace for my troubled mind, and it has stuck with me since that liberating phone call to Bill.

The road to recovery from Vietnam took on new meaning and hope with Jesus in my life.

CHAPTER 13

Making Peace with Your Past

★ ★ ★

I AM A VIETNAM VET who is still affected by the war. I have been struggling with this problem ever since I returned from my tour in '68. When I arrived home, I tried to return to normal life, but my war experiences had blocked off my emotions.

I was twenty when I got home, and the Army made no attempt to debrief or counsel me. As a result, I was discharged with many unresolved issues that I have only amplified over the years.

I held many jobs, did a lot of drugs, and drank a lot to help me repress things, but things just got worse and worse. I got married to a beautiful woman, and she put up with my state for eleven years. After having a lovely daughter, things got really bad for me again. I became more and more depressed, my relationships with this beautiful person and child began to fall apart, I became a stranger to her—paranoid, isolated, suspicious, and withdrawn.

My job got bad, too. I began to experience fits of rage, flash-backs, and doing bizarre things. I was soon fired as being in-competent, and despite the love of my family, I deteriorated into a shambling hulk, and soon the inevitable happened—they left me.

I am increasingly suicidal at this point. I have become cyni-cal, paranoid, and depressed. I search for a way out of this, for a path to take to peace, a way to a new life. But I have almost given up.

My parents strive desperately to help me, trying to pre-serve what little I have left. I sought help from the Veterans Administration, and I have been handed around from one so-cial worker to another, from one psych ward to another, from program to program, none of which has addressed itself to my problem.

Where does it all end for me? What is going to happen to this veteran's life?

I would appreciate any direction you could supply. Please stay in contact with me. What is available in my area from your ministry?

—A Vietnam veteran, thirty years later

The above is an actual letter received at the headquar-ters of Point Man International. It is typical of the kind of correspondence our organization receives on a daily basis, from literally around the world. Point Man is one of a few veteran outreach groups in the United States designed to help you with your specific problems from the war.

I invite you to contact one of the Point Man outpost leaders via our international headquarters. They would love to meet you, and I believe that through Point Man you can find freedom from your memories of Nam and from other PTSD symptoms. Let them point the way to a new freedom through Christ. The rest of this chapter explains why you should contact them.

WHAT IS POINT MAN?

PMI is an international, nonprofit, veterans-for-veterans agency. Point Man provides a support-group setting where you can meet with other Vietnam veterans and finally let down your emotional perimeter. It also provides a safe harbor for Nam vets who have been down the same trails and understand where you're coming from.

The weekly group meetings emphasize a family atmosphere. They know that many Nam vets will open up, or accept counseling, only from other Vietnam veterans. The brotherhood is based on our shared experiences. You can trust them because Point Man is run solely by Vietnam veterans.

Secular counseling procedures are avoided on the most part. It is no secret that many of you have been run through the gauntlet of government programs and are fed up with the runaround they've given you. Our sessions are different. Our first concern is to help you develop trust again. Each meeting is begun by identifying each other, what unit we were in while in Vietnam, what year or years we were there, and what we are doing now.

When I mention trust, it really boils down to our strategy. As brothers, we "watch each other's back" while opening up after so many years of holding the hurt inside. You have probably not been able to talk with anyone about the war for years. At a Point Man outpost meeting, you can sit down with a bunch of guys who are not going to criticize you. You can listen and watch, without being expected to say or do much of anything. In time, you will feel relaxed, because you'll recognize you've finally run into a group of guys who understand you and express genuine concern for you. They won't give up if you explode in rage, or cry, or walk away. They've been there too.

Point Man is made up of Christian veterans of the Vietnam War. But it does not pound you over the head with the Bible. Your interest in restoring your own life is what will motivate you to find freedom and victory. Point Man will prod gently to help you open up and let go of your memories and pain. The outpost leaders will treat you with respect, friendship, and love. They rely on God and pray for you in the process.

Nothing is charged for the outpost services because we trust God to provide all our funding through gifts from people and companies that see the importance of helping people like you. Point Man does have conferences, and only minimal registration fees are charged; you have already paid the price for the war.

The key to our success in helping veterans is that our primary strategy is confession. You probably immediately think of confession as telling someone, such as a jury or police officer, about the wrong you have done. This kind of confessing gets you locked up, punished, and ridiculed publicly. Nobody wants that. Why tell someone something you've done when all you're going to get from it is more misery and suffering, right? But there is another way to think about confessing.

In previous chapters, I wrote about "stuffing" our memories and other ways we repress or hold in our feelings of hurt, pain, and despair from our experiences in Vietnam (and from returning home). The fact is that we can only hold them inside for so long before they explode, through fits of rage, violence, or self-destructive behavior. Like physical wounds, psychological and emotional wounds have to be cleaned out before they can heal. And you clean these kinds of wounds by dumping, letting it out, confessing the pain, hurt, anger, sorrow, terror, and remorse. A Point Man outpost meeting provides the safest environment in which to do this. You can finally talk about the horrible things you witnessed, did, or failed to stop while in Vietnam. No one will judge you, because everyone is there to find healing for himself, and to help others in the process. The security of knowing that every man in the group has probably done similar things during the war will help you be honest with yourself and others—maybe for the first time since the war. That will help you cleanse the wound.

JIM, A NEW GUY IN THE GROUP

In order to help you picture what to expect at a meeting, let me tell you about Jim, a Vietnam veteran who visited one of our Seattle outposts.

It was a rainy Monday evening, which is common in Seattle. Our weekly veteran's group had just gotten underway, and the air was a bit electrified by the pounding, monsoonlike downpour that drummed on the small office complex in the northern suburbs. Some of us were remembering the rain in Nam.

The outpost leader, Gene, was his usual smiling self. His teeth shone through his Paul Bunyan beard, and he was eager to get into a Bible study he'd been preparing all week. The new guy, Jim, was nervously sipping his coffee. His eyes flickered from one veteran to the next, searching for a safe reference point. Not knowing what to expect, or what these guys would be like, he had come dressed in a sports coat and tie. Occasionally, he reached up and loosened the tie in an attempt to fit in with the seven casually dressed men around him.

Gene began the meeting by introducing himself, naming his unit in Nam, when he was there, and how his week had gone since they had last met. The introductions proceeded around the table until it was Jim's turn to speak.

"When were you in-country, Jim?" Gene asked

"I was in Nam from '66 to '67," Jim said.

"What unit were you in?"

"The first division up by the 'Parrot's Beak.'" Jim paused. He seemed a bit confused. Then he went on, "You know, I don't know why I'm here. I've tried every vet help group there is, and I've pretty well given up on . . ." He broke off and began to sob into his hands.

Rich, another veteran, placed his hand on Jim's shoulder. "It's OK, brother, you're among friends, and we love you, man."

Jim looked up and gathered himself together a bit, nodding an OK to Rich. "Sorry, sometimes it feels like I got a big pool of something that just boils up inside and then out it comes."

Mel joined the conversation. "Yeah, I know what that's like. I couldn't cry for fifteen years. I didn't even cry when my mom died. Then one time, I went to an air show and an F-4 Phantom buzzed the airfield real low, you know, and I just broke and cried for about three days. That was about the time I found these guys, and well, I know why I broke now, and I've found out that crying is a pretty healing thing."

"This pool you mentioned, Jim," Gene asked, "what is it exactly? Can you describe it?"

"It feels like a slow-motion movie of a bunch of newsreels all jumbled together, and it really makes me sad. But sometimes I get mad when I see them in my mind."

"Are there nightmares, too?" Gene asked.

"Yeah."

"What do you normally do to control these 'movies'? Do you have any way to turn them off?"

Jim answered immediately. "Yeah, I drink. Booze numbs me. I've spent a lot of nights sitting in my dark kitchen with a bottle of Jack Daniels. It really keeps things from boiling over, and the nightmares don't bother me at all."

"What was it in Nam that got you the most?" Rich asked.

"I don't know if I really want to talk about it, OK?"

"That's fine," Gene said. "We can move on. But there's one thing that I've found out in this group, and that is that revealing is healing. Most of us have been down the same trails you have. We've done some pretty rotten things and had some pretty weird experiences in Nam. And we just want you to know that it's OK to let it all hang out here, because there ain't no one going to judge you."

Gene turned to Mel. "How are you doing this week?"

"I'm still sober. It's been six weeks since I went on a binge, but I can't say I haven't been tempted. Whew! It's a hard hill to hump. I do have a little good news to report, though. A couple of weeks ago I had a dream—a nightmare, I guess. I was sitting on a night perimeter in the bush. It was raining, but the air was real misty. You know how it used to get up in the highlands. Suddenly, I could smell the gooks, and I knew if I could smell them, they were real close. Then a trip flare went off, and out of the night, three of them jumped in the hole with me and started dragging me off.

"I woke up panting real hard, and I was drenched with sweat. I got up, and normally I would hit the bottle to numb my brain; I just couldn't go back to sleep for fear that that stupid dream would continue. But I did something unusual. I got down beside the bed and prayed to God that He would take every dream away from me. I asked Him to just let me sleep until morning. I really felt relaxed when I did that, and I rolled back into bed and fell asleep almost immediately and didn't wake up until nine the next morning. A simple thing, but, man, it worked."

"That's great," Gene said. "Sometimes all it really takes is to give a little more than we ever have before, and giving in to God is certainly a big step for a bunch of hard-heads like us, right?"

Most of the men laughed, and the group lightened up.

"I think that's interesting that you had a dream like that, because I frequently have similar ones," Jim spoke. "But I haven't done anything about it except get drunk. I think the toughest thing for me to deal with was the kids over there. What a stupid war!"

There was a long pause. "What about the kids, Jim?" Gene asked.

Jim was silent for a long time. "What a waste," he exclaimed in frustration, and began to cry again.

The group was quiet. In time, Jim began to talk again.

"I was a medic. I was supposed to save lives, and here I was getting off on shooting people." He began to sob again. "Once in the Iron Triangle I was part of an LRRP team, and we ran into a village that had just been visited by the Viet Cong. The place was still smoking. In the village yard, there was a pile of kids' arms that they had hacked off because a Green Beret medical team had been through and inoculated the kids for cholera a few days before. The damn VC had cut off their arms to teach the village a lesson in not taking anything from the Yankees, including medicine." Jim began to cry again.

"What did you do, Jim?"

He was quiet again, for a long time.

"I went crazy. I lost it. I started shooting every—" He broke again. "I shot a bunch of people—" He slumped forward on the table and let the tears run. A couple of the guys went over and put their hands on his shoulders, sobbing with him.

Gene spoke again. "Jim, you gotta know, brother, that we're in this thing together. There's no way you can pack that kind of stuff around alone. Believe it or not, God didn't do that to you, and He really does love you. It was a terrible place to be when we were younger, and all those memories that have been stuffed inside need to be cast upon someone else's shoulders. Someone who is willing to share your load. God wants to take that rucksack off and carry it for you, brother, but you first have to be willing to give it up. He ain't going to take it if you can't give it up."

Jim was still sobbing, but he replied, "This is the last stop, man. I've tried everything that I know how to do to get some peace, but it isn't coming. If I don't get it here, well, I've had it. I can't go on."

"Can we pray with you? Will you pray with us?" Gene asked gently.

Jim answered, his head still bowed. "Yeah, I gotta do something. I'm ready to give it up."

They prayed together as a group.

This story illustrates what I mean when I say you need to confess your experience to get it out. It isn't easy. After so many years of keeping up an emotional perimeter, it's hard to let it down. But like Jim, me, and the Nam vets in the meeting that night, you can let it go—if you want to bad enough. Our outpost leaders will prod you, but we won't push. We'll love you as a brother and watch your back for however long it takes, because we know that you want to be free and it is God who can give you that freedom. He gave it to me. He gave it to Bill Landreth, the man who started Point Man in 1984. And he has given it to thousands of other men and women like you since.

CHAPTER 14

Triggers, Tripwires, and Booby Traps

★ ★ ★

INCREDIBLY, THE GROUND WAR *was over in 100 hours. Buzzards spun in patient circles overhead and wild dogs scavenged through the sand of the Iraqi desert. I'll never forget the detail I pulled burying the bodies of the enemy to keep the critters from getting them. It was a lonely and thankless task.*

We searched each body for identification and placed it, with any photos, money and other personal effects, into plastic bags and hung them as best we could on sticks or under rocks on top of the graves. Then we wrapped each soldier in whatever we had, (usually a blanket or the chemical protection suit that each Republican Guard soldier owned), and laid him to rest.

This war has been called a war where "smart weapons attacked and destroyed dumb targets," and thousands of Iraqis gave up and surrendered. We lost so very few, and it was a war where everyone on the winning side was a hero. Our home-

coming was quite a celebration. But I don't feel like I did any-thing to deserve a hero's welcome.

I have trouble sleeping now, and sirens and other city noises keep me on edge. When I hear a fire truck go by, I want to look for shelter, thinking that something's going to explode nearby.

Even though we didn't fight much over there, I still think I've got some nerve problems, or something. I don't dare tell anyone about it because I'm afraid they'll laugh at me, or tell me, "You don't deserve to have a problem from your war experiences—remember, you won and we gave you a parade when you got home?"

—A US Gulf War infantryman

The Gulf War was a stressful time for most Vietnam-era veterans. We saw the shades of some familiar dark clouds begin to form on the horizon. The old specters of political grandstanding, military ineptness, and human wastefulness seemed to reach out from the endless, dramatic CNN news-casts and wrench our guts. We began to get the old feelings of helplessness as we watched our young military—some of our own sons—being marshaled for combat. It could have been *us* all over again. Fortunately the president was wise enough to leave the fighting up to the warriors. Two significant Vietnam veterans—Generals Norman Schwarzkopf and Colin Powell—did a splendid job. They kept things from turning into the never-ending nightmare that we went through in the sixties and seventies. Yes, there is a God who hears prayer.

Yet the Gulf War did have an ongoing effect on me and on many other Nam vets, and it caught us by surprise. Sur-prises and I don't get along—even to this day. My purpose in writing this section is to alert you to some possible reac-tions that may happen along the march, especially when new wars break out.

HOW I BECAME A CASUALTY OF THE GULF WAR

I was preparing for a trip to Reno, Nevada, when the Gulf War first broke out. I had been invited to speak at a Vietnam veterans' conference and was getting my things together for it. At that time I usually wore my jungle fatigues and boots when I spoke at such events, and the TV was on while I packed my clothes. I absorbed the extensive live coverage on television and watched with the rest of America as the tracers lit the night sky over Baghdad and reporters described the incoming missiles with fear in their voices.

Without realizing it, I lost touch with present events and slipped back to the night of May 5, 1965, when was I packing my things on Okinawa to be deployed into the Vietnam combat zone. Athena, my wife, was the first to notice that something was wrong; wives usually are.

I had become angry, short-tempered, nervous, and hyperalert. I lost my usual easygoing demeanor and became overly demanding. The preparation of my suitcase was methodical and disciplined to a fault. I had become a focused, calculating machine. Packing became a serious, life-or-death activity. I exerted so much control in what I was doing that I was out of control—and scary to be around. Everyone in the house had to walk on eggshells to keep from rubbing me the wrong way

Fortunately Athena had been ministering to people with PTSD long enough to recognize my newly reemerging symptoms. She sat down and helped me through this time of confusion and disorientation. When I finally realized that this new war had caused my reaction, we actually had a good laugh about it. But for a while we were both caught off guard. I knew that we had crossed a new bridge, not only in our marriage, but also in our ministry in helping others.

What had happened? Simple. Do the math with me. The extensive, live war coverage on TV, plus packing my old army duds, plus preparing for the "mission" equaled a post-traumatic stress reaction. I didn't recognize the signs along the trail, and walked right into a "future war" ambush.

Since we were in a ministry for veterans at the time of the Gulf War, we heard many similar stories from around the country. We heard about Vietnam veterans trying to reenlist to go to war again. I even heard of one Vietnam vet in Virginia who committed suicide after he was turned down by an army recruiter to go over and join the fight.

The war in the Gulf also affected me in that I made some very bad decisions in my work at the time. I would never have thought a war that I was not involved in could influence me as much as it did, but I do know that war's effects can turn small problems into huge issues.

I became a casualty of the Gulf War in a strange way. Not long after the war ended it seems like I, too, had ended something, and I stopped doing what God wanted me to do, which was to help veterans through Point Man Ministries. I used many excuses for spending my time doing other things, but I was really running away from the very thing that I was supposed to be doing.

I have, by God's love and mercy, regained some of the battleground that I lost back then by working as a chaplain for veterans. I also know that my writing continues to help veterans so I keep at that, too, and occasionally I get an opportunity to speak to veterans and on behalf of veteran causes. However, I am still making up time lost because of my own reactions to a war that I never fought in.

Based on my own reactions and on those of others, I've realized the need for Vietnam vets to watch out for situations and events that can unexpectedly trigger a reaction. We have to be watchful and alert, and we have to have others watch with us. Conflicts and wars around us can unexpectedly trigger unwanted reactions, but if we are prepared we will have more control of each situation.

WARNING SIGNS

Just like in our military training, exercising and practicing certain methods kept us ready for things to come. Now it is time to implement some new methods to be ready. This method is to recognize the signs that either cause or contribute to stress. If we stay alert and know the signs, we will have a better time of managing those things that lead us into ambushes. Here are the primary signs we need to watch for:

1. Allowing ourselves to become overly fatigued
2. Low concentration or focus
3. Lashing out in anger for no reason
4. Changing eating and sleeping habits
5. Using alcohol and drugs

TRIGGERS—THE MENTAL AMBUSH

Trigger is the term used to describe those events and reminders that cause veterans and other trauma victims to respond adversely because of their past experiences. When a particular traumatic incident occurs, it is imprinted and stored permanently in the mind. What makes these subconscious memories especially harmful is that they continue to cause stressful and inappropriate reactions when stimulated by triggers in our present environment.

To better manage our post-Vietnam lives, it is vital for us to learn as much as we can about our own triggers. By knowing more about what sets us off, we can move in the direction of gaining control over tense and potentially harmful moments and situations.

A classic example of a triggered response is when a combat veteran who has arrived back home suddenly dives for cover at the sound of fireworks on the Fourth of July. The explosive sound tells his brain that he is under fire. The brain, unable to differentiate between a real or imagined threat, signals the person to react. The vet naturally responds by instantly going into combat mode. That old imprinted message in his head told him to move into action and survive!

When the brain receives a smell, sound, or any combination of some fifty other sensory perceptions that may be associated with a past injury or threat, it compels the person to react—and unfortunately most of the time it is an *inappropriate* response. When this happens, the veteran suffers tremendous emotional pain, fear, helplessness, and confusion. Those close to him are affected too, and they do not understand. They feel frustrated because they cannot relate or help him end his pain.

Once while attending a veterans conference on the East Coast, one veteran shared a most interesting trigger with us. He could never figure out why he lost it every Tuesday morning. He happened to be working the midnight shift at his job, and usually got home just before the garbage trucks made their pick ups in his neighborhood. His family always expected him to be in a bad mood on these particular mornings and walked on eggshells until he went to bed (if he could). When he began to become aware of these triggers he realized that the large, black, plastic trash bags lined up along the streets were a subconscious trigger, reminding him of the many body bags he had seen and handled in Vietnam. Once the trigger was discovered by both him and his family, they could begin to deal with it in a positive fashion.

ADRENALIN

Adrenaline is at the root of the trigger and PTSD problem. Created and imparted to us for survival, adrenaline is a God-given quick-response mechanism that helps us avoid danger—or fight it. When a trigger gets activated, the adrenal glands secrete survival hormones into our system. This sudden flow of hormones gives us the flight-or-fight response to danger. However, the brain doesn't know when it is a real threat or a past memory that is being restimulated from an incident in our minds. In either case—real or imagined—adrenaline flows, and we generally react to survive.

Since our reaction to these triggers can be dangerous to our health—as well as to our relationships with loved ones, friends, and others—identifying and evaluating triggers is a critical first step in gaining victory in the area of post-traumatic stress and adrenaline surges.

IF YOU CAN'T FLEE OR FIGHT, YOU MUST ADAPT

During wartime, we could respond to danger by either fighting or fleeing—but when we're having coffee at Starbucks, it's just not acceptable behavior to do either. Now that we're in civilized, peacetime society, we must learn a third option. We have to learn to adapt or adjust in response to triggers, instead of fighting or fleeing.

A vital key to learning how to adapt is to *become aware of what sets you off* and triggers your adrenaline. It's also very important for family and close friends to learn these triggers. It's always better to stand guard with a buddy.

Each time something in the environment stimulates an adrenaline surge, practice doing the following:

1. Write down on the Trigger Chart on pg. 161 what was happening when the trigger was pulled. Then

write down the exact trigger. Record your immediate response to the trigger. Then try to recall the original incident, the memory, that the trigger is acting on. Then share this with a friend who will understand and relate to what you are sharing.

2. It's vital to share your list of discovered triggers with your wife and children. They will begin to understand you and your experiences better. Hopefully they will learn how to help you through the process by becoming more aware of what sets you off.

3. Realize that triggers, PTSD, and your traumatic experiences are too big to handle on your own. Share your list with a buddy or support group of peers. And finally, but most importantly, do your best to pray and ask God to help you carry these burdens. Nothing is too big for Him to handle if you are faithful to allow Him the freedom to intervene for you.

4. After one month of logging your daily triggers, look over your chart and note the triggers that have bothered you frequently. Then begin an attack campaign on those areas. Zero in and work with a buddy to learn how to recognize and avoid those trigger points if at all possible.

The following chart is a tool to use in identifying and recording triggers. However, it is *not* the answer. The answer lies in God, who desires for you to be liberated through Him. He wants you to live a life free from the enslavement of post-traumatic stress. This chart will help you map out the areas that you need to deal with at once, and then those you eventually will have to handle. Do not be surprised to discover some triggers that you were not aware of. And don't be overwhelmed by the number of triggers that may appear on the chart over a period of time. All triggers can be disarmed and rendered harmless with a good support unit—and don't leave God out of the process.

TRIGGER CHART					
DATE	EVENT	TRIGGER	RESPONSE	RECALL	MIND

1 Date—Record the date that the trigger was activated.

2 Event—Record the event in which the trigger was pulled, such as "I was alone in the dark; I was in Chinatown; it was a rainy night," etc.

3 Trigger—Record the actual trigger, such as "A helicopter flew over; fireworks suddenly went off nearby," etc.

4 Response—Record your immediate response to the trigger, such as "Fast action into combat mode to survive the threat, fear, anger, surging blood pressure, crying, urge to run away," etc.

5 Memory Recall—Try to recall the original traumatic event with as many details as possible. These events can be feelings, emotions and decisions that occurred during the high stress of an impacting incident. An example could be remembering what you did under enemy fire.

6 Self-Triggered—Record a check mark in the "mind" column if you triggered yourself with imagined or assumed threats to survival of self and others, as opposed to having your environment trigger you.

Throughout the process, be sure to pay close attention to repeated triggers. It's the repeated triggers that you need to deal with first. You will be tempted to give up, but don't. Stick with it.

As you go through your daily routine, keep this chart handy and try to record the times you get triggered. Each person has his own triggers that have developed throughout his lifetime, and it's true that we learn not to put our hands on hot stoves once we get burned by one. Life is a growing process, and surviving is a learning process, so by recording these triggers, we can begin to get a handle on them in the future.

The Missing Step in Coming Home

★ ★ ★

IN THE YEARS SINCE VIETNAM, most of us have already taken a number of steps away from that first day back in the world when we got off the airplane. When we got home and unpacked our duffel bags, we discovered we had a place to put most everything—except a year of our lives that didn't fit anywhere.

Where do you put things like perimeter duty and walking point, incoming and medevacs? What do you do with the anxiety of never knowing what would happen next, the pain of losing close friends, the emotions of anger, fear, hatred, love, terror, and boredom that made up the Vietnam experience? And more significant still, to whom do you talk about something that nobody understands?

We've taken a lot of steps away from those years, but there have been rough times for us all, and there are still more steps to take. I went to the VA in 1989 and filled out the paperwork to see if I had PTSD, and I realized that in the fifteen years after I got back from Nam, I'd been through two divorces and sixty-five jobs. I never blamed Vietnam, but then I spent many years in denial too.

We survived. That was the first step.

A Wall was built in Washington and it began to heal a nation. We were able to affirm ourselves through it. That was the second step.

And we reached out to help our brothers. That was the third step. We found other vets, we got into rap groups, we went to Vet Centers, and some of us found Point Man Ministries along the way. By 1986, I found myself with a group of other Vietnam veterans, sharing our experiences and shedding tears we'd been holding back for over twenty years.

Many of us have continued reaching out to others: homeless vets, jobless vets, incarcerated vets, vets with PTSD, POW/MIAs and their loved ones. This step has made a big difference. Point Man International Ministries, The National Conference of Vietnam Veteran Ministers, Vets with a Mission, Victory for Veterans, and other helpful programs have been a major part of all these steps: helping us survive, reaching out, healing a nation, helping others. That's good. And yet there is another step to take and we must be bold enough to take it.

For most veterans, in one way or another, God was a casualty of the war. The typical religion we learned as children was often made up of mostly innocence, optimism, and enthusiasm.

It was made of elements, such as "Have a happy day!" and "Everything will turn out all right," with a little "The good get rewarded, and the bad punished." And perhaps the most important of all, the idea that you can cut a deal with God: "Live right, say your prayers at bedtime and God will keep nasty things from happening to you."

That kind of religion seems harmless until something nasty does come along. And for a lot of us, Vietnam was very nasty. If we thought we had a deal with God, God failed the test, and we've never forgiven Him for it.

And so we have another step to take, and the challenge is this: to open our eyes, look around us, and see—truly see—what there is to see. Look at life over the past thirty years and see the points at which there has been healing, the points at which someone has believed in us, the points at which there has been a helping hand, the points at which someone has stuck with us even when the going was difficult.

There is no doubt in my mind that each of us has had an experience like that since coming home from the war. I say we have been experiencing the grace of God. However, something has held us back from recognizing it, and it has everything to do with the step that was missed when we returned home.

What is God's grace? Grace is the forgiveness God gives, not because we deserve it but simply because He loves us and is faithful. His grace allows us to have salvation and healing through His Son, Jesus Christ—new life that lasts through all eternity. Jesus paid a debt He didn't owe, a debt we owed but could never pay ourselves.

The idea of a grace period has special meaning to vets. That's the time a creditor gives us after the bill is due. When I went to Vietnam I really didn't expect to come home. When I landed there in 1965 I figured my bill was due, and if the bill collector came, so be it.

When I got off the plane in San Francisco a year later there was a piece of me that was a little surprised. I'd received the gift of an extension of my life, even though it took me over two decades after Vietnam to appreciate that.

I'm living my life in a grace period now. My life is something given back to me after I'd kissed it off. Maybe you can identify with that as well.

You don't have to be religious to experience God's grace; it's free for all, whether you can figure out what's going on or not. But I am confident that He will continue to give us clues to what *is* going on. And to the extent that we take the next step and open our eyes and hearts, we will never be the same again. You just need to know, if you can't be free from the past, you will have a hard time finding the future.

So let's talk about the next step that God is offering us today. I believe it is a step that was missed along the way, and it is long overdue. The moral needs of soldiers returning from Vietnam were often overlooked by American society. The country as a whole simply chose not to take seriously the moral pain felt by many young soldiers when they returned home.

Moral pains of shame and guilt were ridiculed or reduced to "psychiatric difficulties." Unlike veterans of previous wars, who came home with their outfit on troopships, we were whisked one at a time from the combat zone and within hours deposited alone in American society. Although we were expected to have some guilt and shame, we were largely expected to pull ourselves up by our bootstraps and get on with life. But our lives could not be whole again because we didn't know what to do with the moral issues of our experiences. Most of us stuffed them back into the duffel bag and figured they would go away on their own. We have found out, of course, that those issues never go away.

I believe that the missing step in our return from Vietnam does not lie in the area of humanistic psychology, but in the realm of the spiritual. We were never given a chance to cleanse ourselves, to purify ourselves, from participating in or witnessing the dirty work of war. And we have been rejected and we have rejected others because of this. Our hearts have not been pure because we have not cleansed our hands.

In medieval times, leaders recognized the need to cleanse and purify their soldiers as they came home from war. Soldiers were required to spend an established time period in purification rituals before they could reenter the community—not as a penalty or punishment, but as a compassionate act of acceptance, healing, and readjustment back to normal life again.

It was a wholesale statement from the community that they were welcome home, they were loved, and they were *needed* to be useful members of society again. All that was required is that they allow the community to join them in purifying themselves from the darkness of war.

The soldiers were required to strip off their battlefield wardrobes, and join with the community in burning them. They would pass all their weapons through a fire to decontaminate them from enemy blood. In some cases they'd pile their swords and shields in a heap and pulverize them to uselessness. All of this was a symbolic act of the community agreeing that "It's over! Now let's get back to living rather than killing." The soldiers viewed it as a normal, necessary step in the process of coming home and being accepted back into the community after serving in war. The Vietnam veteran never got his purification ritual. He never had the opportunity to take off his war clothes, burn his weapons and be embraced by a loving community of those he fought for.

If we feel that we never got the support we deserved, then it is time to take the next step. I encourage the folks in the community to put some effort into recognizing, loving, and honoring a Vietnam veteran. It can be a simple thing. At a Promise Keepers convention in Atlanta recently, a speaker mentioned Vietnam and asked the Nam vets in attendance to stand. The vets, expecting polite applause, were stunned as 60,000 men gave them a ten-minute standing ovation. Every vet was repeatedly hugged and thanked for his service. You may not have 60,000 men in a stadium, but somehow let your community's Vietnam vets know that they are truly home—that you want them in your life. Encourage them to use their talents and skills to make a better world to live in.

It works both ways. Vets, let down your guard and allow those in the community to express their thanks for the sacrifice you paid while in their service. But most of all, I ask you to let go of the bitterness and unforgiveness that has bound your soul. Forgiving people, governments, celebrities, the military, protesters, and family can be the best healing ointment you will find. This final step in coming home may be the toughest step you will ever take, but it is worth it. Forgiving someone takes a lot more courage than charging an enemy bunker, or walking exposed across an open rice paddy.

Forgiving those who have wronged you is a subtle, yet powerful cathartic healer. Let me tell of one episode where I saw its power in action. I was a speaker at a national conference for Vietnam veterans and their families. My topic was anger management, but the subject of anger took my talk in a direction that I never expected. During the question-and-answer period, someone expressed his hatred for a Hollywood actress known better for her vocal and active opposition to the Vietnam war than for the quality of her acting.

I asked for a show of hands of those who had never forgiven this particular celebrity. Nearly every man in the room shot his hand in the air; some even held up both hands to punctuate their feelings. None wanted to forgive and forget. Uncertain what kind of reaction would come, I cautiously broke some news to them. I announced that I had decided to forgive this person and to release her from the captivity I had kept her in. I went on to say that I realized there was nothing I could accomplish by hating her any longer, and I chose to let it (and her) go.

I then told them how I felt that if I continued not to forgive her, then I was having a "relationship" with her that I didn't want to have. The unforgiveness locked me to this person, and I had no control over it. By thinking of her, and holding onto the anger and hatred, I was creating my own shackles of bondage. Consequently many of my fellow veterans attending saw that they, too, wanted to be free from this person in the same way.

Many were set free from a booby trap that day. Unforgiveness was that trap. Their lives, like mine, have taken on new wholeness just as a result of simply letting the woman walk out of our lives for good. We, as a group, then prayed corporately and forgave this person.

I don't see many miracles in my life, but that day I did when one particular marine veteran forgave this celebrity. This man had been wounded by a .50 caliber round, and was paralyzed from the waist down and in a wheelchair for more than two decades. By a simple act of faith, he forgave this infamous woman, and within a couple of hours was out of his chair for the first time in twenty-three years. He stood and walked away from his wheelchair that day, never to return to it. For some reason only known to God, that bitterness and unforgiveness was keeping him bound to a life without walking. Now I can't say the results will be so dramatic for everyone who forgives, but I do know that I saw the pure, raw power of God acting positively on behalf of a person who gives up his own grudges and lets *the* higher power take command.

Forgiveness remains a mystery to man, and it takes great courage for us to make that quality decision to forgive. But if you decide to carry through with it, I know your life will never be the same again.

"Welcome home" is a signature phrase used by many Nam vets, but "welcome home" takes on a new meaning for us when we not only make peace with our pasts, but when we also make peace with God.

The mention of God, the Bible, or Christianity is a turn-off for many Vietnam veterans. As I mentioned in an earlier chapter, some believe He went AWOL and turned His back on them, or that He is very evil to have allowed what we saw and experienced there. He no longer deserves our faith.

Like most recruits, many of us went overseas with deep religious impulses. We believed in God and expected Him to be good, compassionate, and just. We thought He would never fail us. That He would lead us to victory over an evil foe, just as He had done in all previous wars this country has fought. We expected Him to preserve us in battle. But we saw things differently in Vietnam.

We all went to Vietnam with some degree of faith, based on either our beliefs or on the Christian principles and morality upon which our country was founded. Many of us lost our faith because we felt we had been had by God, our country, and our leaders. We felt that God was somewhere else while we had to witness and be exposed to horrible things. So we blamed Him.

I can remember praying like mad during incoming mortar attacks or firefights, and then getting up off the ground afterward and saying to myself, *Well you pulled your-*

self through another one. Never once did I give credit to God for having saved my life, even though I had prayed furiously during the heat of danger. And that's the point.

The majority of the teenagers who went to Nam became spiritual casualties. After spending long months in that world of crime, prostitution, murder, and humping through nearly impenetrable jungles, we began to recognize the dark side of our human nature. This awesome potential for evil terrified our teenage minds into a new rationality about life. The typical "grunt" infantryman became accustomed to living on an animal level. To believe that God loved us was difficult because of what we saw and how we had been trained.

Many soldiers claim that in basic training they were taught how to be animals. "They take you down, tear you apart, and put you back together again piece by piece, the way they want you to be. You are taught not to think, but to react. You're taught to be an animal. Then you're expected to suddenly forget your training as an animal after the war. I know how to act like an animal. I don't know how to be human anymore."

Our training began the process of dehumanizing us. It removed God's basic gifts to us: love and caring for others. First we lost our trust in emotions, replacing it with repressed rage (enough to enable us to kill) and with social isolationism. Trained to take life, we reentered a society whose foundation was "Thou shalt not kill." We couldn't jibe this with the senseless death and killing we had seen in Vietnam. So we stuffed our God-hate feelings along with all the other pains. And we confused nationalism with God's favor, expecting Him to give us victory because we were Americans.

God did not go AWOL in Vietnam. In fact, He was there suffering with us. He kept you alive and brought you back for a purpose. But you won't discover that purpose until you make peace with Vietnam and with God. Point Man can help you do this. Contact them. They will help you take off your rucksack of pain and return to living life as you were meant to. This is my invitation to you: Find the true meaning of "Welcome Home." Reach out and find a new brotherhood; call Point Man International (800) 877-VETS.

> I think you ought to know, dear brothers, about the hard time we went through in Asia. We were really crushed and overwhelmed and feared we would never live through it. We felt we were doomed to die and saw how powerless we were to help ourselves. . . . (2 Cor. 1:8)
> —Paul of Tarsus, Point Man, A.D. 65

To order additional copies of

Making Peace with Your Past

Send $10.99 plus $3.95 shipping and handling to

Books Etc.
PO Box 4888
Seattle, WA 98104

or have your credit card ready and call

(800) 917-BOOK